T0195003

Out on Your Own

Starting a Private Practice for Mental Health Practitioners

Kerry Heath, LPC, CEDS

WESTBOW
P R E S S®
A DIVISION OF THOMAS NELSON
& ZONDERVAN

WestBow Press books may be ordered through booksellers or by contacting:

WestBow Press
A Division of Thomas Nelson & Zondervan
1663 Liberty Drive
Bloomington, IN 47403
www.westbowpress.com
844-714-3454

ISBN: 978-1-6642-8792-1 (sc)
ISBN: 978-1-6642-8793-8 (hc)
ISBN: 978-1-6642-8794-5 (e)

Library of Congress Control Number: 2022923789

Print information available on the last page.

WestBow Press rev. date: 01/24/2023

Contents

Note to Reader

I would like to disclose that I am not in any way affiliated, sponsored, or receiving any monetary compensation for mentioning any companies, organizations, or products within this book. They are merely examples of products available to utilize and are not to be considered endorsements. Any perceived slights of persons or organizations are not intended.

The information contained within this book is accurate and up to date to the best of the author's knowledge at the time of publishing. It should be noted that local, state, and federal laws change frequently and vary greatly between disciplines. Each insurance contract is unique to the parties involved.

This book is provided as a guide for professionals and should not be used as a replacement for consultation with attorneys, accountants, licensing boards, insurance companies, or any state or federal agencies. All practitioners must adhere to local, state, and federal laws regarding the operation of their businesses as well as regulations related to any professional licenses.

The author assumes no responsibility for omissions, inaccuracies, misinterpretations, or inconsistencies herein. Readers should not substitute this book for legal or financial advice from qualified professionals.

Introduction

If you're considering starting a private practice and you decided to purchase this book, congratulations on making the perfect first step! You've already achieved your first goal in opening your own business. It is my intention to answer as many questions as possible that anyone considering starting a private practice might have. If you already have an established practice, there may be a few nuggets in here for you as well. At this point in my life, I don't attempt to put together a bookshelf without reading the instructions first because I have learned that figuring out the process from those who've gone before me is the quickest route between points A and B. Can I put the shelf together on my own? I can eventually, but it will involve a great deal of wasted time, frustration, and possibly injury or added expense while I figure out how to complete the task. I believe that starting a new business is the same. Seeking wise counsel is the best place to start.

I ought to begin by sharing a bit about myself so you know who you are accepting advice from. I have worked at all levels of care including at a nationally renowned inpatient treatment center for eating disorders, where I spent nearly eight years as a therapist and an assistant clinical director. I have owned a private practice since early 2011 in several states. I have primarily specialized in the treatment of eating disorders, OCD, and trauma.

In 1998, I earned a master's degree in marriage and family therapy from Oklahoma Baptist University. Additionally, I have a bachelor's degree in business administration from the University of Tulsa. At the beginning of my career, I worked at an adolescent group home and then at a preadolescent inpatient unit and day treatment program while attending graduate school. I then moved into therapeutic foster care before working at a private practice in 1998 in Tulsa, Oklahoma, along with my LPC supervisor.

I first owned a practice in the Washington, DC, area before relocating to the Phoenix, Arizona, metro area. I currently reside in Arizona with my husband and two children. I enjoy homeschooling my two children, traveling, and writing for an online therapy web site and various online magazines.

Starting my first private practice was like being pushed out of the bird's nest in a way. I had been laid off from a hospital administration job in Virginia while on maternity leave. This left me feeling overwhelmed and in quite a bind financially. Once I was able to return to work, I ended up managing a community mental health agency. I quickly realized that this was not an ideal position for a new mother. I needed something with more flexibility. Job dissatisfaction and a desire to spend as much time with my children as possible were what I needed to venture out on my own.

I had only a vague idea of what went into starting and operating a business like this. I had very few people in my life to ask for help. I feared losing my health insurance. I was afraid it would take longer to generate income than I could afford. There were days that I told myself I'd never have any clients at all. I reached out to a few colleagues who had already made the leap into private practice. Due to what I hope was simply busyness, they were reluctant to offer much assistance. I was unable to get any help with the steps to take, how much to charge, how to create my forms, or where to rent office space.

Now that I have been in private practice for over two decades, I realize there doesn't seem to be a shortage of clients. There is no reason to keep the process a secret. Therefore, I am writing this book. I want this information to be available to anyone who wants to venture out on their own. We have a shortage of providers. We need all the practitioners we can get. I don't want anyone else to feel as helpless as I did when I began this journey.

Taking the first steps to leaving your nine-to-five job with benefits and heading out on your own can be scary to be sure. There aren't graduate courses in most counseling programs that teach us how to start our own businesses. There are so many things to consider that if you haven't done it, you wouldn't know that it needs to be done. It can seem daunting. I think it is helpful to hear from those who have been successful. A road map of sorts that outlines all the things in order of importance. It can be done. Once you get started, it will all be worth it. Private practice isn't for everyone. For me, it has been the best decision. It has improved my health. It has benefited my family, and it has given me a sense of professional accomplishment that I never achieved through any other job.

If you think it is for you, I encourage you to read through these chapters. I suggest grabbing a notebook so that you can take notes as to what you will need to do to begin your business. Highlight things that you want to come back to later, and feel free to use any of the example forms that I provide within the book.

Getting Started

Types of Practices

I am writing this book from the perspective of someone who has worked in the mental health field for three decades. I am going to share my perspective and experience after having practiced in three states. I am not a lawyer, nor am I a financial advisor or an accountant. Nothing in this book should be taken as legal or financial advice. I intend for this book to serve as a reference or starting point that you might get if you were talking to a colleague who had been in practice before you. I hope there are portions that you will find helpful. There may be portions that do not fit for you. That's how it works when you talk to a colleague and seek out advice. You take what fits and leave the rest.

The hardest step is deciding you are going to start a private practice. I made the decision after working several dead-end jobs following being laid off from my *dream job* while on maternity leave. Yes, you heard that right. I was laid-off from a job with a newborn and had no job prospects. To make matters worse, I was on disability due to complications related to a difficult pregnancy and birth. So, I was very underemployed and unhappy. This does propel one to do scary things. It is easier to risk a loss of income when you've had a significant drop in pay already. The main concern I had, though, was losing my health insurance with two small children. That was my first task. I had to find a way to get health insurance. This may or may not be an issue for you. Fortunately, as is often the case in life, God provided this at just the right time. My husband was offered health insurance through one of his professional organizations just as I was losing mine.

I knew I wanted to work with like-minded individuals after not having that privilege for a few years. I have never been one to wait for opportunities to come knocking on my door. Starting my private practice was the same way. I looked online to see who was practicing in my area. I saw a few who were treating the patient population I wanted to treat. I sent letters asking if they wanted another experienced therapist to join them. I also specifically looked for Christian counselors. There were very few practices advertising for new therapists. I didn't let that stop me. I sent out an email to the practice I most wanted to join. And by the next week, I had an interview with them. I truly believe God led me to them as they were preparing to advertise soon after they received my inquiry. I started my first independent private practice less than a month after sending that email to them. You don't have to wait for a job posting. This won't work every time you are seeking out a practice to join, a specific position, or office space to lease. However, in most cases, people do appreciate those who take initiative and put out effort for what they want. You can make your own path toward where you want to go in life and your career.

Business Models

The first choice I made was whether to join an existing practice or to venture out on my own entirely. The choice made often depends upon one's licensure status, but not always. There are some states that allow those who are not independently licensed to own or even practice as a counselor without an onsite supervisor in their own private practices. I am biased against this model for many reasons, but nobody asked me. There's plenty of time for owning a practice after you've had some time and experience under your belt, but it is legal in some states. Two other options are either working in a group practice or owning your own practice as an independently licensed practitioner.

Group Practices

Many clinicians work in group practices first. This takes away many risks involved and provides supervision opportunities for those not yet independently licensed. In most cases, there are two popular scenarios when joining a group practice. For those who haven't been working long, it may be wise to join a practice that offers services to you for a portion of your fees collected. The second option is to rent office space, along with other therapists in a group practice, while remaining an independent practitioner. Due to the unknown, I began my private practice journey with the first model. I had no idea how long it would take to establish a case load. I didn't know anything about billing or how to deal with insurance companies. It seemed attractive to me to have some assistance, even if I had to give up a percentage of my income to pay for these services.

I joined a well-established Christian practice in a community near my home. I paid a percentage of my monthly income to help pay for two secretaries who provided several services to me. At the time, the going rate was between 30 percent and 40 percent of a therapist's monthly earnings in most cases. This percentage also rented me a furnished office to use exclusively to see my clients five days a week. This was not the exact office I would have chosen but sharing the expenses of an office is more affordable than paying for an office all alone—especially before you have established yourself as a therapist in your community. Had I known it would only take a few months, I may have gone out on my own, but none of us has a crystal ball. It is a risk either way. I knew that having a fancy, well-decorated office was not nearly as important to me as seeing clients and getting my business started. The experience I gained at this practice was invaluable.

It was nice to have a secretary to help me get paneled with insurance companies, to schedule my intakes, answer the phones, check in clients for appointments, and to do all my billing. I was also permitted to utilize office equipment and basic supplies. This reduced my startup costs as well. I didn't need to purchase supplies, a printer, a billing program, or other furniture. All these things can be done independently. I do them all now for myself with no issues. Office expenses will be addressed later in the book.

Joining an established practice may be a good way to begin for those who do not have an established niche or specialty as well. The practice will be able to provide a new therapist with intakes and referrals based on their established reputation in the community. Essentially, the advertising is done for you. You may not have a great deal of control regarding which clients you see, however. This will have to be negotiated prior to signing any contracts. The pressure of filling your calendar is lessened with this method of starting your practice.

Solo Practice

The second option is to venture out on your own. You can do this solely on your own, or you can rent office space with other clinicians who also want to practice independently yet want to share expenses. I have done this as well. It does cut down on the overhead of rent. It also provides a nice practice experience for the client. They have larger waiting rooms, more people around, which adds to safety, and maybe even a receptionist. I have also rented a private office all on my own. Any of these options are perfectly fine. It depends on your financial constraints, connections in the community, and personal preferences. My most recent business model was to go in on office space with several other clinicians and work out of my home as I primarily conducted telehealth sessions during the 2020 pandemic. That will be addressed in chapter 9.

I intentionally sought out a group of like-minded, Christian practitioners to share space within this instance as well. While working as an independent practitioner separates your businesses, you are working alongside everyone in the shared space. These are the people you will utilize as consultants, share the restroom with, and negotiate daily housekeeping tasks. Can you trust that these counselors will run their businesses in an ethical fashion? Will they treat your clients well when they see them in the waiting room? Are they going to treat the shared space in a respectful manner? Can you count on them to manage incoming mail with confidentiality? They are essentially professional roommates. If their businesses are doing well, that helps your business as well. It is wonderful to have trusted colleagues in your office to refer to when your practice is full and vice versa.

Business Model

You will also need to decide how to structure your business. You may decide on a sole proprietorship, an LLC, or several other variations. I suggest consulting with an accountant and/or a lawyer to determine which structure you feel may work best for you. Regardless of your structure, you will also need a business bank account, a debit/credit card, and probably checks. I have all three of these set up for my business account. I rarely write a check, but it is necessary occasionally.

You will need to consult with the city where your office is located to determine whether you are required to apply for and maintain a business license. Usually, the fees for this are nominal and will likely be paid each year to renew the license. This is different from your professional license. I have had offices in areas where I was required to do so and in areas where I was not.

You will select a business name. You will want to ensure the name you have selected has not already been chosen. There are various web site builders that sell domains so that you can search for and then purchase a domain for your web site. GoDaddy and Wix.com are examples of businesses that offer this service. You will also want to make sure you follow any state and federal guidelines regarding the naming of a counseling business. There may not be any restrictions, but you will want to make sure. There are some who use their name in their business name, while others prefer not to. This is a matter of personal preference. If you do not use your name, you will be *doing business as* (DBA) the name you select such as Right Start Counseling. Jane Doe is doing business as Right Start Counseling.

Sole Proprietorship

I would say that roughly half of the people I know choose this option. It is the most basic of the ways to structure your practice. In a sole proprietorship, you are responsible for the business as well as all assets and liabilities as you are the only owner of the business. Many new counselors begin with this structure as it is simple and inexpensive compared to the other options.

Limited Liability Company (LLC)

Each state may have different regulations regarding how to start an LLC. This business structure does offer some level of protection in terms of individual liability as well as some tax benefits. Many counselors choose to structure their businesses this way. Those that I know who do not go with a sole proprietorship have opted for an LLC in most cases. It is not available in all states, however. An LLC does cost more to start and maintain than a sole proprietorship. It is wise to consult with an accountant and an attorney to discuss the pros and cons in terms of taxes and liability.

S Corporation (S Corp)

This type of business structure is taxed on a personal level. I do not personally know many counselors in this category. Those who have chosen this are able to save on self-employment taxes, yet there are fees and regulations involved due to the requirements of shareholders. There is some advantage related to less liability.

C Corporation (C Corp)

This structure allows for multiple owners and is not limited to US shareholders as in the case of the S corp. This structure is preferred by investors. This is generally reserved for large companies.

Insurance Panels or Private Pay

O nce you have selected where to practice, the next step is to decide whether you plan to accept insurance payments or not. There are pros and cons to becoming contracted with one or more insurance companies. I decided to accept insurance payments for services. It is wise to start the application process at least a month before you plan to begin seeing clients if not sooner. It has been my experience that this step is one of the lengthiest of the entire process. If you are depending on insurance clients to fill your practice, it will be difficult to fill your weeks until you are paneled. Some of the companies paneled me within thirty days while others took up to six months.

Prior to applying to be a provider for an insurance company, it is a good idea to have various things collected to save yourself time. You will need a copy of your license and malpractice insurance. You will also need to apply for an NPI (National Provider Identifier) and CAQH (Council for Affordable Quality Healthcare) number if you have not ever done this prior to opening a private practice.

You can apply online for your NPI by visiting the National Plan and Provider Enumeration System (NPPES) web site. This web site is https://nppes.cms.hhs.gov/. You can also call 800-465-3202 to speak with customer service.

Most insurance companies require a CAQH number as well. You can get a number at the www.proview.caqh.org web site. CAQH is a database for insurers. Theoretically, they access this database to credential providers and update provider profiles. My experience is that you will be required to update this database throughout the year at predetermined intervals and each insurance company that you are paneled with will also require that you attest to your provider information multiple times each year even if nothing has changed. Because both steps may take several weeks, you need to add this to your timetable. You will also save yourself aggravation in the future if you have your office address prior to registering for both numbers, but especially the NPI. This is not absolutely necessary, but to prevent future problems with reimbursement from insurance companies, do not forget to change the primary address associated with your NPI if you move your practice. Any time you move your practice location, you will need to update your provider profile information with every insurance company you are contracted with either online or by mail.

The next step is to determine which insurance panels you wish to apply to work with in your area. There are a few strategies to consider. There are some who focus on one or two big companies while others work with as many as possible. I chose the latter when first starting out because that was the way the practitioners managed their business at my first practice. This isn't the worst way to begin for several reasons. The first is that you have a much larger pool of potential clients to receive referrals from the more insurance companies sending them to you. The second is that they will not all have your contracts prepared at the same time. It is likely that you will begin your practice with only a few of these contracts in place.

The following is a list of most of the insurance companies that I have been contracted with at some point in time to give you an idea of what's out there:

- Aetna
- Anthem
- Blue Cross/Blue Shield
- Carefirst
- ChampVA
- Cigna
- Empire Blue
- Humana
- Kaiser
- Magellan
- MHN
- Tricare
- United Health Care

You will find that rates of reimbursement will vary depending on which insurance company you are contracted with, your credentials and areas of expertise, as well as geographic area of your office. Some insurance companies will not allow additional providers onto their panels in certain zip codes if they determine that the area is saturated with providers. I have been able to appeal this by having a specialty area of practice, which I will address in chapter 4. It has been my experience, however, that regardless of where my practice has been located, the need for providers has always outweighed the supply. I can only speculate as to why these companies limit the number of providers on their panels. At any rate, I have always been able to work with any insurance company or EAP (employee assistance program) that I desired to.

Employee Assistance Programs

At times, you may be asked to enroll as a provider for an EAP associated with a commercial plan that you are contracting with. They may or may not give you the option. This isn't always a bad thing, but there are some things to know about EAPs. In general, there can be more paperwork involved in providing services to clients using their EAP benefits. An EAP is a service provided through an employer. This program offers their employees free and confidential assessments and short-term counseling and/or referrals who are dealing with personal and/or work-related problems. A client usually receives anywhere from three to nine sessions, depending upon the company providing the insurance. This is where the additional paperwork can enter the equation for the therapist. If you have a client with three sessions, you may have an initial packet to complete upon admission. After three sessions, you will likely complete more paperwork to refer them out, or more likely to extend their care with you. This continues every three sessions into infinity in most cases. The evaluations required are more cumbersome than with traditional insurance companies as well. After all the additional work on the part of the therapist, some insurance companies reimburse at a far lower rate than they do for the exact same service if paying you under the commercial insurance portion of your contract. Conversely, there are some EAPs who do pay quite well. You will discover which ones you enjoy working with and those you do not after only a brief time if this is something you decide to do.

Private Pay

There are advantages to a cash-only or hybrid practice that includes at least some private pay clients. This is the model that I have chosen for myself. A private client is one without insurance who pays a flat fee for the services provided. It is up to you as the provider to set your fees in this case rather than accepting whatever fee the insurance company dictates you are worth. One advantage to this is that every hour you work is reimbursed at the same rate. This is helpful when budgeting. When only accepting insurance clients, it is difficult to know whether your case load will be comprised of the highest reimbursement rates or mostly the lowest. If the range is large, this can make a significant difference from month to month. When only accepting insurance, your hourly rates will vary according to which insurance companies you are working with. For example, there was a time that my hourly rate varied from $60 an hour to $112 an hour. This was quite a few years ago before I learned to negotiate my rates. Yes, you can negotiate your rates with insurance companies if you have something to offer them. I now have a much tighter range so that I am better able to budget what my intake is likely to be each month according to how many sessions I have scheduled. We will discuss setting rates in chapter 7.

As a Christian counselor, you may also find that local churches add you to their referral lists. They often cover the costs of their members to seek out counseling and then pay you directly for your services. This will fall under the private pay category as well. They may limit the number of sessions that they will cover like an EAP. Once a client has exhausted those services, they may then utilize a commercial insurance plan or wish to continue treatment with you based on a predetermined cash rate.

Marketing, HIPAA, and More

If you know my background, you might expect this chapter to be lengthy and full of grand advice. I do have a bachelor's degree in marketing (BSBA). To be completely honest, though, most therapists do not have to spend a fortune to advertise much at all to keep their practices full. There, I said it! When I started out, I did all the marketing things. I mailed out postcards, I hosted groups, and I bought fancy pens, business cards, referral forms, etc. Nope. Not necessary. That's not to say that you might not get a few clients from those efforts, but the return on your investment is minimal. I do recommend buying business cards, signing up for an online therapy directory, and building a web site at the minimum. I like to get business cards that have the feature to write the client's follow-up appointment on the back. This is a nice way to give your client a business card at each session to hand out to others along with a written reminder of their next session. I personally buy mine at Vista Print, but there are plenty of affordable places to purchase these. I made the mistake of paying far too much my first year or two for business cards. This is not necessary.

Multidisciplinary Treatment Team

In 2015, I moved my practice from Northern Virginia to Phoenix, Arizona. I had a waiting list within the first six to eight months. The only formal *advertising* I did was to maintain my web site and profile on an online therapy directory. Now the other thing that is important is to establish a network of providers that you refer to and work with as a multidisciplinary team to treat your clients. I immediately located psychiatrists, family practitioners, registered dietitians, and other professionals to form a team to treat my clients. This is crucial for the proper care of your clients and provides a built-in referral base. This may or may not be able to sustain your practice. It truly depends on the volume of clients your team sees and the patient population you and your team are serving.

Online Therapy Directories

I do suggest an online therapy directory as well. There are several popular ones to choose from that provide a regular flow of referrals. Many of these provide a free trial period so that you can get a feel for the service prior to paying a monthly fee. Your listing on a therapy directory can be linked to your business web site as well. I find that those who do this are viewed as far more professional than those who do not. Some of the more reputable sites include

- Psychology Today
- Good Therapy
- Therapy Tribe
- Therapy Den

Web sites

Designing a web site can be a challenge. There are several ways to go about achieving this task. You can pay someone to do this for you or you can do it yourself. I went with the second alternative because I had no idea the first option existed in 2011 when I was opening my practice. I think it is critical that the web site looks professional. This is an expense that you may want to incur if you aren't especially gifted in this area.

Email

A HIPAA-compliant (Health Insurance Portability and Accountability Act) email to use for your business is necessary for your practice as well. I personally use Proton mail. There are many options available to choose from as a clinician. You will want to make sure that you can obtain a BAA (business associate agreement) from any vendor you choose to ensure your contractors agree to keep your client's information secure. You will need to ask prior to hiring any vendor whether they offer a BAA to therapists. Some other email providers that advertise that they are HIPAA compliant are

- Hushmail
- NeoCertified
- Mail Hippo

Faxing

Sending and receiving faxes is another part of the electronic portion of your business. It is helpful to have this set up prior to printing your business cards. You can have the traditional fax machines that utilize an actual machine and a landline, or you can use a HIPAA-compliant service that does not require a phone line but is an online service. Sfax and eFax are examples of this service. They are HIPAA-compliant services and offer a BAA for their users.

Relationship Building

Reaching out to other professionals in the community who interact with your clients on a regular basis is also a good strategy for marketing your business. For example, if you treat children and adolescents, school counselors, psychologists, pediatricians, and psychiatrists are a good place to start. Introductory letters letting these individuals know that you are opening your practice and what conditions you treat may begin a long-standing working relationships and referral sources.

When opening a new practice, you can utilize one or two of these strategies or all of them. It has been my experience that focusing on just one or two in the beginning is the best use your limited resources. It also allows you to better track which strategies are bringing the most clients to your practice. This can and likely will change over time as well. In the beginning days, a therapist directory and insurance panels may generate the newest client phone calls whereas in later months and years, word of mouth and professional referrals may be the best sources of your new clients. This all depends on the efforts you put into marketing and growing your business in the beginning. Hard work initially will pay off in the end. The best marketing is a job well done.

Generalist versus Specialist

Establishing a specialization is an important way to differentiate yourself from other therapists in your community. It provides exceptional marketing opportunities as well as a sense of professional fulfillment for most. It makes sense that if you are one of only a few practices offering treatment for OCD, for example, you will be in a unique position as a professional. This is even more true if you are also providing OCD treatment for children from a Christian perspective. The more specialized you are, the more selective you can be regarding clients you accept into your care. You can also determine whether you want to accept insurance payments versus private pay based on personal choice rather than financial necessity. You are likely to maintain a waiting list rather than spending your time thinking of new and better ways to drum up business. If you have decided to advertise that you are a Christian counselor, you have already established one specialty that is truly important and unique in our profession. I have also found that many families have a difficult time finding Christian counselors who are able to treat the conditions they are dealing with in their communities.

So what is a specialization, and how do I choose one?

The first question to ask is whether you desire to specialize in something. Becoming a generalist is not a negative. It is crucial to know how to treat most any condition that presents itself to you in private practice. A specialist is not one who does not have competence in most *general* conditions. Why is this? Take my primary specialty, for instance. I specialize in the treatment of eating disorders. I also treat children, adolescents, adults, families, and couples. I must also know how to address mood and anxiety disorders, OCD, personality disorders, and other childhood disorders such as ADHD. You get the point. I cannot treat an eating disorder without a fairly good grasp of most mental health conditions. I do not see many of the serious mental health conditions that are presented at the community mental health center that I worked at for a short time, however. Do I recognize them if I see them? Of course. They are not my specialty, though. A generalist, however, can recognize OCD, anorexia, or selective mutism. They are not likely adequately trained to treat an individual with one of these conditions unless they have established a specialty in doing so. A generalist will need to refer these clients to a specialist.

Most therapists establish specialties due to having acquired experience working with a particular population of patients. A student may work with children during a practicum or internship and determine that they enjoy it. The work experience gained at a first job may lead to gaining subsequent jobs working with the same population repeatedly. Over time, a therapist becomes an expert by virtue of years of experience. If a person works at a drug and alcohol treatment center right out of graduate school, they may develop a specialty in this area for this reason unless they conscientiously decide to change to another patient population. At times, a therapist knows what population they would like to work with, and they seek that out as their first job to gain work experience. Those who work in environments where there is a wide variety of diagnoses are more likely to remain generalists unless they deliberately seek out a specialty based on a condition that they enjoyed or felt they were especially skilled at treating. One advantage of becoming a generalist is that some people may find that it provides more variety and therefore they may be less likely to develop burnout. It is true that some of the more difficult to treat specialties can and do lead to burnout more often if a clinician is not cognizant of this possibility.

Either way, there is no best way to practice. It is a personal preference that most do not decide on right out of school. It is best to look at what clients you connect best with and are enthusiastic about meeting. Ask yourself what conditions elicit passion in you. This is likely the specialty that will be a good fit for you.

CHAPTER
FIVE

Multidisciplinary Treatment Teams and Referral Sources

There are many reasons to practice as a part of a multidisciplinary treatment team. The first is that it is best practice. This ensures that your clients receive a combined level of expertise from a range of professionals in the community. This provides the most comprehensive and holistic approach to your clients' conditions at the lowest level of care possible in most cases. Teams are comprised of professionals with complementary skills with similar treatment philosophies and goals. Teams can consist of many disciplines, including counselors, primary care providers (PCP), psychiatrists, dietitians, occupational therapists, and school counselors.

With a private practice, you will encounter patient scenarios in which consultation with other professionals is necessary. There are decisions regarding treatment and how to manage potential dangers that require second opinions. It is nice to have other professionals who are already familiar with your client and their condition and circumstances. It may seem exciting to be able to make your own independent decisions. It is most of the time. It can also be scary to be the only one solely responsible for decisions that greatly impact the lives of others. This is especially true when a counselor is treating children with serious conditions that require medical treatment and/ or hospitalization. This is also true of conditions that relate to a person's faith background. In recent years, many children have come into my practice presenting with gender dysphoria, for example. It is helpful to be able to speak to other Christian counselors regarding how they are integrating faith into the treatment of the LGBTQ+ community in ethical and respectful ways. This is a delicate issue when we are treating children of one declared faith and parents of another, for example.

A second reason that it is helpful to practice as part of a multidisciplinary treatment team is that there is a built-in referral network of trusted individuals for your practice. It is equally as important to have trusted referral sources for your clients as it is to have incoming referrals for your practice. For instance, I work with eating disorders. I would not be nearly as successful at treating my clients if I were not able to refer to competent dietitians, PCPs, and psychiatrists in my community. We all treat various aspects of the disorders and work closely together to restore our clients to health. I am not able to prescribe medication or address nutritional issues. If the members of my clients' teams were not a part of a team, the treatment philosophies may not be similar. This has the potential to be quite detrimental when/if the treatment of one professional may be undermined by the recommendations of another who makes opposing suggestions. This can be especially problematic when working with children and adolescents whose parents are relying on the teams to make treatment recommendations for extremely ill children. Regular communication and established trust are crucial when working as a team to treat patients as a team.

Usually, you will find that there is one member of the team who takes the lead position with any given client. It may be the professional who first encountered the client. Some teams have an established way of handling critical decisions. I have been a part of teams in which the medical doctor, or PCP, tends to be the lead. I

have most often been a part of a team in which the therapist and/
or dietitian tends to make the final call about treatment decisions.
This may be due to their levels of expertise in treating eating
disorders related to other team members. Regardless of how a team
is structured, it is crucial that all members are respected, listened to,
and honored. Each member of a team provides a valuable perspective
to both the team itself and to the client and their family.

Regular communication and collaboration are crucial to
providing quality care. It has been my experience that professionals
who work within treatment teams tend to have far better treatment
outcomes than those who work independently. Clients can remain
at lower levels of care when each treatment provider is reinforcing
treatment goals during each client meeting with both the client and
family. There is better follow-through and accountability. No one
person can meet the needs of a client. Also, if each team member
is working independently, there is less consistency in holding the
client accountable and seeking out assistance in reinforcing concepts
being taught. When a client is struggling to accept a concept, for
example, it is much easier if heard in several places than just from
their doctor or therapist, but not from anyone else. They can easily
dismiss it as something that one person believes to be true but that
is not factual. In treating eating disorders, we all assist one another
like this. We attempt to normalize eating three meals a day, taking
medication that has been prescribed, and looking at people as others
see them. All three professionals—the psychiatrist, the RD, and the
therapist—work together to relay these messages rather than each of
us driving home our own message independently. It is much more
impactful.

Scheduling and Billing

Scheduling and billing are important aspects of running any private practice. There are several ways to approach these tasks. You may have these tasks done for you if you join a group practice that has hired someone to perform these duties. The first practice I had was set up like this. We each contributed to the salaries of two different office staff who answered our phone, checked in our clients, scheduled our intakes, verified insurance benefits, and billed for services rendered. As a new solo practitioner, this was very helpful. I had no idea how to bill to insurance companies or what it took to keep a practice full. The office manager had a much better idea of how many clients I needed to see each week to earn a particular salary. She was able to teach me about insurance companies, how to get paneled with them, and how to complete claims forms.

Scheduling

Eventually, I learned that scheduling was something that I preferred to do for myself. I do know many counselors who use their electronic health records (EHR) for this purpose. I will address that a bit later. I am old school when it comes to scheduling. I prefer to have the old pencil and paper calendar that we used to see at the doctor's office over an electronic one that clients access to schedule their own appointments. There are many reasons that I prefer not to hand over this control to someone else. A computer program cannot differentiate between a client in crisis and one who tends to schedule for more social reasons than true clinical need, for example. I may prefer not to have two family sessions or acute eating disorders back-to-back due to the tendency to run long. I cannot program this into my calendar.

I like to schedule intakes at certain times versus follow-ups. Every clinician will have to determine these things for themselves. I have found that most clients prefer to have standing appointments scheduled versus varying days of the week and times. This also makes scheduling easier for me. Another benefit to this form of scheduling is that I can have a master schedule in which I can easily see openings in my schedule and availability for new intakes. I have always blocked off a few time slots each week that are dedicated exclusively for new intakes and others that are reserved for established clients. For example, my new intake time slots tended to be Tuesdays and Thursdays from 11:00–12:15. Occasionally, I would open one or two afternoon times when I found that I needed to fill several openings at once. For those who are not overly particular about their schedules, this may not be an issue. Every clinician will have to determine these things for themselves.

Billing

Billing is another business task that a counselor can pay someone to do for them or learn to do for themselves. Many EHRs also perform this function. I do not use my EHR for this either because I do not use it for scheduling. Generally, the billing is attached to the scheduling and documentation components of the EHR. The first time I was in practice, I gladly allowed the office manager to handle this task. I was blissfully unaware of what was involved in billing for my services. I turned in my calendar each week and received checks from various insurance companies each month. It was easy.

The second practice I owned, I hired someone to do the billing as a private contractor. This proved to be a negative experience. I ended up having to redo a great deal of the work I had paid my billing agent to do. Mistakes delayed me getting paid. They also caused issues between me and my clients. Clients were often upset over receiving bills that they really didn't owe due to the billing agent's mistakes. I learned, though, through addressing each of the errors. While this did not work out for me, several of my colleagues have gone this route with great success. It obviously depends on the individual you hire and their level of competence. Get several references if you plan to go this route.

Once I opened my third practice, I was convinced that I could manage the billing on my own. I decided to give it a try rather than paying someone else a portion of my monthly income to do it. Once I learned how to submit my billing, I realized that it really didn't add much time to my day at all. I had a better grasp on what was billed and whether the claims were being paid. I was better able to answer clients' questions regarding their insurance benefits. It has turned out to be a good thing for my business. I have far fewer insurance denials now that I do my own billing. Truthfully, I rarely have services denied anymore. The only things I really wish I still had someone else to do are answer the phones and verify insurance benefits. Maybe it's just phone work that I don't like.

To manage the billing for yourself, there are a few things to learn. Whether you input billing information into your EHR or into an online clearinghouse, such as Office Ally or Availity, you will need to familiarize yourself with what is called the CMS 1500 claim form. This is the form that is used to submit claims to insurance companies. Diagnostic (ICD-10) and CPT (Current Procedural Terminology) billing codes are required to submit these claim forms. The most frequently used CPT codes are 90791, 90834, 90837, and 90847. These are used for the diagnostic evaluation, individual and family therapy. There are some differences among insurance companies regarding which CPT codes are reimbursable and which ones require prior authorization. Counselors will need to become familiar with the organizations they are contracted with and verify coverage for their clients prior to providing services. There are fees associated with using products that require CPT codes as of 2022. Practice management, EHR, and billing clearinghouses will all collect annual licensing fees on behalf of the American Medical Association (AMA). Each professional will have to pay each organization a fee annually to utilize these required codes for billing purposes. These are essentially royalty fees for the use of these codes. A practitioner cannot file insurance claims without using these codes. This added approximately $18 to each of the products I paid for beginning in April 2022.

Setting Rates and What Services to Offer

One of the most frequent questions I get and the hardest for me to get answered when I first started was this: how much should I charge? The short answer is this: whatever you want. You get to decide how much to charge for the services you provide. There is a bit more to setting rates than determining what you'd like to make at the end of the month, however. The way I went about it was to conduct a bit of a market survey. For some reason, the people I knew in private practice were a bit closemouthed about certain aspects of starting their practice. Their fee schedule was one of those things. I went online and tried to find as many counselors' web sites that listed their fees as I could to get an idea of the going rates in my geographical area. I compared my education, years of experience, and level of expertise to those therapists and adjusted accordingly. To be honest, you want to set your rates at a reasonable level. You don't want to be the cheapest or the most expensive in your area. If you are taking insurance reimbursement for your services, your rates are not going to have a lot of bearing on your income anyway.

Another factor in determining how you set your rates is the number of clients that you intend to see each week. This is especially true for those who choose not to contract with insurance companies. For example, if you determine that you would like to earn $75,0000 per year, you first must decide how many weeks you'd like to work. Maybe you want four weeks off for vacations and holidays. That leaves you forty-eight weeks to earn your $75,000. You must then earn $1562.50 each week. If you charge $200 per session, you must see approximately eight clients each week. This is, of course, before taxes and expenses. I would increase the number of clients you estimate needing to see each week of your first year or two until you determine your expenses, tax obligation, typical number of *no-shows*, and how often you tend to get sick and need to call off work. I have included a form to calculate income and expenses in the appendix.

How do you determine what services to provide? Well, most counselors provide individual therapy. The question is whether you will provide family, couples, or group therapy as well. Also, what age range are you going to serve in your practice? Adults only? Will that include the geriatric population? Will you accept Medicare? Will you treat children? Adolescents? Do you have experience treating families? Do you have training in these areas? Will you offer any specialty groups? Perhaps a women's group? A grief support group? A teen group for self-injury? A DBT group? Will you offer all these things right away or gradually add some as you grow your business?

I have done all the above. I have offered individual, family, couples, and group therapy. I have treated age four through one hundred. As I have aged, I have dwindled down the things that I offer in my practice. I have gradually eliminated one thing at a time as retirement gets closer and closer to be more easily prepared to close my practice at some point. I have gone from being open five days a week to four and then to three. I have gone from seeing age four and above to ten and above and then sixteen and older. I no longer facilitate groups for lack of time in my schedule. I refer my clients to others who are doing groups. I rarely supervise anyone anymore. I am preparing to pass the torch to the next generation of therapists.

Something else that providers need to be aware of is legislation related to requirements regarding providing good faith estimates for out-of-network and private-pay clients. The following is taken directly from the cms.gov web site:

> As of January 1, 2022, consumers have new billing protections when getting emergency care, non-emergency care from <u>out-of-network providers</u> at <u>in-network</u> facilities, and air ambulance services from out-of-network providers. Through new rules aimed to protect consumers, excessive out-of-pocket costs are restricted, and emergency services must continue to be covered without any prior authorization, and regardless of whether or not a provider or facility is in-network.
>
> Previously, if consumers had health coverage and got care from an out-of-network provider, their health plan usually wouldn't cover the entire out-of-network cost. This left many with higher costs than if they'd been seen by an in-network provider. This is especially common in an emergency situation, where consumers might not be able to choose the provider. Even if a consumer goes to an in-network hospital, they might get care from out-of-network providers at that facility.
>
> In many cases, the out-of-network provider could bill consumers for the difference between the charges the provider billed, and the amount paid by the consumer's health plan. This is known as <u>balance billing</u>. An unexpected balance bill is called a surprise bill.
>
> The Consolidated Appropriations Act of 2021 was enacted on December 27, 2020, and contains many provisions to help protect consumers from surprise bills, including the No Surprises Act under title I and Transparency under title II. Learn more about <u>protections for consumers</u>, <u>understanding</u>

costs in advance to avoid surprise bills, and what happens when payment disagreements arise after receiving medical care.

These policies are likely to change, and counselors need to keep apprised of these and other regulations related to their practices. Most licensing boards and/or professional organizations do send out notices about policy changes in advance of them taking effect. This is a good reason to be a part of a consultation group. There may be things that other professionals hear about that may slip by you. For those clients who choose to utilize out-of-network insurance benefits or pay cash for your services, you may choose to provide a superbill so that they can submit claims on their own behalf. An example is provided in the appendix.

Paperwork and Electronic Health Record

As anyone who has worked any amount of time in the mental health field can attest to, paperwork is one the most time-consuming aspects of the job. This is, sadly, one thing that follows us to private practice. There's just no getting around it. Paperwork in your private practice will fall into two basic categories: documentation and forms.

We are all accustomed to documentation. We have been told since day one, "If it isn't documented, it didn't happen." We've attended training after training regarding the importance of timely and accurate documentation. This is true in private practice as well.

The second type of documentation is forms. If you have worked at an agency, a treatment center, or hospital, the forms were already in place when you arrived as a new employee. You were expected to utilize them and become familiar with the forms your agency used. When you open your private practice, there are no forms waiting for you. This is another area I found was a closely guarded secret when I asked around for advice before opening my practice. You are in luck. I am sharing all my ideas with you! You have my permission to use whatever you like and leave the rest. I have always shared with my colleagues. There's no reason not to.

So back to documentation. Most people in 2022 have some version of an electronic health record. I use one. I have looked at and tested many of them. To be quite honest, I do not like most of them. There are aspects of most of them that I dislike so much I won't subscribe to them. I do not find them to be user-friendly. They are a necessary evil. What I do like about them is that they provide a professional-looking progress note and initial assessment to provide to other professionals when needed. There are instances when a counselor must provide records to other professionals, whether it be a court, an attorney, another therapist, a doctor, etc. I find that a typed-out record looks more professional than the handwritten ones of decades ago. Therefore, I pay the monthly fee to have access to this way of documenting my sessions. This also makes storage easier. There is far less paper involved if you are documenting electronically. I tend to have a hybrid medical record, but many have transitioned to a completely electronic version.

There are many options when it comes to selecting your EHR. Cost and options play a role in which one you may choose. Some of your other products may offer discounted rates on an EHR as well. Your therapy directory, the malpractice insurance company you use, or a professional organization may offer discounts. Here is a list of some of the most popular EHRs. I am not affiliated with any of them, nor am I endorsing any specific product.

- Simple Practice
- Therapy Notes
- TheraNest
- TheraPlatform

There is a learning curve regardless of the product you choose. Each one has a unique set of features that you will want to practice using prior to getting started. The more features you use to run your practice, the more familiar you will need to be. Some of these products schedule, bill, accept credit card payments, and allow you to document everything that you do along with providing a telehealth platform. Some EHR products are HIPAA compliant, and others are not. This is another aspect to consider. You will want to obtain a business associate agreement (BAA) with your EHR and all other companies that have access to your PHI. I believe that the four EHRs listed provide a package that is HIPAA compliant and will supply a BAA when asked. This may change after publication so you will need to research this if you choose one of these products.

Prior to opening your private practice, you will need to create all your patient forms. This can seem overwhelming, but after just a short time in practice, it will be evident what you will need. There are many ways that you can handle this aspect of your business, but some sort of intake packet is needed. You can ask your clients to complete this packet electronically or in your office prior to their first session. An intake packet will need to include several components. Each client must sign a consent for treatment. You will need to provide a copy of your HIPAA policies. They need to be given a good faith estimate of the expected charges and describe your financial policies. You may also choose to have them complete a patient history prior to meeting with them the first time so that you can prepare for their first session. Any office policies that you would like to share with your clients, such as your no-show policy, illness or inclement weather policy, the procedure for dealing with an emergency, confidentiality issues, etc. I also have an adolescent and child agreement. If you provide telehealth, a consent form for telehealth is needed.

I am providing all these forms along with other common practice forms in the appendix of this book for your reference. Each counselor will determine what forms work for their practice and patient population as well as what is required in the state they reside in for their licensure. The forms provided in the appendix are for reference only and are not intended to represent absolute requirements, nor is it an exhaustive list of forms that will be used during one's career. It is important to ensure that any policies and forms are explained clearly and in an easy-to-understand fashion. Counselors should provide clients with an opportunity to ask questions.

In Person or Telehealth

P rior to the year 2020, it never occurred to me to provide telehealth services. In fact, when clients asked to have online sessions, I turned them down, feeling as though it wasn't a wise choice for eating disorder clients. I have since then had a complete change of heart. Obviously, this was out of necessity. I do make exceptions to this based on level of acuity and whether a client has a full treatment team. As a rule, I do not agree to see an eating disorder client who refuses to agree to work with one of the RDs I collaborate with if the need arises. I insist that my clients sign an eating disorder treatment agreement prior to beginning therapy with me. There are eating disorder clients who are stable enough to be in outpatient therapy without the need for an RD. That is beyond the scope of this book.

In today's environment, the choices available to new therapists are limitless. A new business owner can have an exclusive in-person practice, an exclusive telehealth practice, or a hybrid practice. I have transitioned to an exclusive telehealth practice for many reasons. The choice is up to each practitioner. I have found that most of my clients prefer telehealth. It is more flexible and allows clients to schedule around work and school much more easily than an in-person model. I am also able to reach clients I wouldn't be able to otherwise.

There have been a few clients who have left my practice in favor of therapists providing in-person care. The limits to my practice have been seeing young children and acutely ill eating disorder clients who refuse to see an RD in person. I will not see a severely ill client without at least one treatment team member seeing them in-person on a regular basis. The other notable exception are acutely suicidal clients, especially when they reside out-of state. I do hold a license in a state other than my home state, so I do provide services on occasion to clients there.

The first nine years of my private practice experience had an exclusively in-person business model. I found that one disadvantage for me was that I got sick far more often providing in-person sessions. I have an autoimmune disorder so seeing children was always risky. Despite having a strict illness policy, people routinely came to sessions sick. Also, prior to converting to a telehealth model, my own children attended public school. They were also exposed to illnesses regularly and became sick. I found that I missed work much more frequently than I do while seeing clients via telehealth. Even if I am not feeling my best, I can push myself to get dressed and walk over to my home office versus driving across town and being at an office all day.

The no-show and late-cancel rates are much less with telehealth as well. I do not get last-minute calls canceling therapy due to flat tires, being stuck in traffic, and running late to therapy. That is not to say that there are not those who forget about sessions or simply do not attend, but it is a rare occurrence. I can text someone when they are five to ten minutes late and they can log on to the session. With an in-person model, they may be forty-five minutes away from my office when they get that text asking if they are going to be at the office soon. It saves me money, it saves the client money, and it keeps the clients in session.

Another obvious advantage to a telehealth model is the lower overhead. I do not have office rent any longer. Many of the business expenses remain the same, of course, but rent is one of the biggest costs. I no longer have a commute either. I am saving on gas and the wear and tear on my vehicle. My health has improved as well. I can eat at home, I sleep later, and I have more quality time with my family. I am now able to homeschool my children, which is priceless.

Some advantages to an in-person model have to do with the level of social interaction and support I received as a therapist. Being a therapist in private practice is an isolating job already. At least when I was in an office with other counselors, I saw people every day during the week. Now I only see them when I go into the office to check my mail. I must be far more deliberate about scheduling social events and staying in touch with my friends and colleagues. There isn't the spontaneous case consultation over lunch or at the water cooler anymore. We must schedule formal case consult meetings or schedule times to talk to one another if we have a case we need to process.

Each clinician will have to make the decision for themselves regarding which model they prefer. A hybrid model may be the best choice for anyone not sure which way to go. A therapist can always conduct telehealth sessions from their office. Another option is to select a day or two each week to conduct telehealth from home while seeing clients in the office the other days. This will give you an idea of what each way is like and how many clients prefer each model. You may save money as well by renting office space only three days a week versus five, for example.

As mentioned in the last chapter, there are a few additional forms to add to your intake packets if you plan to see clients via telehealth. It is important to know the rules and regulations in your state as well. There are CE (continuing education) opportunities available to educate counselors as to the nuances regarding this type of therapy. As with anything new, it is important to be competent prior to delivering any services.

Malpractice Insurance, Credit Cards, and Other Business Necessities

Nobody likes to think about being sued, but you must have malpractice insurance. Many professional organizations offer discounts for various companies who sell insurance for mental health providers. Professional liability insurance will be a large expense regardless of where you purchase it. Depending upon your lease agreement, you will be required to purchase various riders to accompany a basic policy. This can include slip and fall insurance, flood insurance, and insurance to cover individuals that you are supervising. You may also want to consider deposition coverage, cyber liability, or licensing board defense coverage. The more riders you add to your policy, the more expensive it is, of course. You will also want to be sure that your policy meets the coverage requirements of your landlord. I have found that the higher limits available are typically asked for in most cases, such as $1 million/$5 million. Insurance may cost from $300 to $800 per year depending on the policy and coverage you choose.

Another service that you may want to consider is credit card processing. There are many available. As mentioned previously, many EHRs offer this as a component of their service. You may want to offer this to your clients. You can also use a separate credit card processing service. Some clients will prefer to pay you in cash or check. It is up to you to set your financial policies for your office. As with all other products that receive and store PHI, a credit card processing company must be HIPAA compliant and offer a BAA. Some business checking accounts offer these while other businesses choose a service like Square.

Especially for telehealth practices, it is helpful to have some sort of eSignature product to capture legal signatures on your practice forms. There are several to choose from, including

- DocuSign
- Panda Doc
- Sign Now

There are also many stand-alone teletherapy platforms if you choose not to utilize one within an electronic health record. A few of those include

- Capterra/Doxy.Me
- Secure Telehealth
- Zoom (HIPAA-compliant version)

Business Supplies and Expenses

There are many expenses to consider when both starting a private practice and maintaining your business. Some of these are one-time expenditures, while others are recurring costs. The items that have been mentioned in previous chapters are part of this list as well as additional things that you may not have thought of yet. The following is a basic list to get you started thinking of the things you will need to purchase at the onset of this process:

Office Expenses

- rent
- movers (startup and change of location)
- furniture (for office and waiting room if needed)
- cell phone
- magazines and books for waiting area
- decorations for office

Office Supplies

- office supplies (sticky notes, paper clips, file folders, labels)
- printer with scanning capabilities
- ink cartridges
- computer
- printer paper
- books
- lined pads of paper for note taking
- clipboards
- pens, highlighters, pencils, erasers
- stapler and staples
- planner/calendar
- notepads
- stationery
- postage
- envelopes
- address labels
- paper shredder
- tissues (I buy these in bulk)
- cleaning supplies
- toiletries
- water

Marketing Expenses

- business cards
- online directory
- web site

Professional Expenses

- professional license
- business license
- professional organization fees
- faxing service
- travel
- CEs
- insurance
- professional services (attorney, accountant, bookkeeper)
- taxes
- credit card processing
- bank fees
- electronic health record
- billing agent or service
- eSignature service

Additional Sources of Income

A s you progress in your career and become more seasoned, additional or passive streams of income may become more desirable to you. As counselors, we sell our time. Our income is limited by the number of hours in each day and by the rates that insurance companies determine they are willing to pay for our services. For this reason, many of us look for alternative ways to increase our salaries.

Many of my colleagues have added what are affectionately referred to as side hustles to their private practices to increase their incomes. Some of these include teaching, writing, supervising, consulting, coaching, or adding employees to their practices.

Teaching and Supervision

I have quite a few colleagues who also teach at the college level while working as counselors. Most do this online, but a few do in-person teaching as well. I have been told that the first year is the most time-consuming while developing lesson plans and acclimating to the new position. Most online platforms require a master's degree or higher while traditional educational settings primarily require a doctoral degree. Other ways to pass on your knowledge and experience to people are through supervision and training. For those who have become experts in particular areas of psychology, conducting trainings or workshops can be a lucrative and beneficial means of expanding one's practice. Supervising recent graduates who are seeking licensure is another way to give back to the profession while earning extra income. Some counselors charge their full hourly rate while others offer a reduced fee for their supervisees. This is an area where I learned the hard way to value both my time and experience. It is acceptable to be compensated for the wealth of experience and expertise that you offer to others. There is a pattern of undervaluing those in our profession. At times, the worst offenders have been us.

Writing

Writing is a popular way for many to supplement income. I began writing while still working at a hospital. I learned quickly that I loved doing it and was compensated well for writing journal articles. This was the beginning of my plans to eventually author books. I have authored countless articles. I have been paid for some and others were for the experience, exposure, and contribution to the field. There are some professionals who choose to blog as well. This can be a wonderful way to educate the public while generating income.

Expanding your Practice

Another very popular way to increase income among my colleagues is to expand one's practice. This is generally achieved through the addition of services and employees. Therapists can hire additional counselors to work for them and make a portion of the income that they bring into the practice. These additional professionals can be W9 contracted workers or W2 employees. Counselors who have grown their businesses from a one-man operation to a group practice of multiple practitioners or even intensive outpatient programs (IOP) take on a greater responsibility in terms of potentially paying taxes and benefits for their employees. This puts the counselor in a managerial position in addition to the counseling role that they filled when they were the only person seeing clients. It is at this point that a business may need to be structured differently. The advice of an accountant and possibly an attorney is advised. The counselor will need to develop company policies and an employee handbook along with employment contracts to protect themselves, the employees, the clients, and the business.

This is a big undertaking for anyone. A great deal of thought must go into the type of business you want, the type of therapists and adjunct professionals you want to hire, and the overall role(s) you would like to play in the running of the expanded business. Do you want to continue to see clients? Do you want to manage the business full-time? Do you want to exclusively supervise the employees and step out of the clinical role of therapist? Are you going to hire others to run the business for you? Do you have colleagues in mind you wish to ask to join your business, or are you going to advertise for the positions? There are many considerations when expanding a practice in this way.

Regardless of the business model you choose or the process you take personally, private practice has the potential to be rewarding both personally and for the communities you serve. Transitioning from working for hospitals and other agencies into owning my own business has been the best decision for both my family and me. It hasn't been without challenges, but I cannot see myself going back. Business ownership isn't for everyone, of course. If you have ever thought you would like to try it, I encourage you to take the steps I have detailed in this book to venture out on your own. I truly hope that you begin your journey in a more confident way. It is a one-step-at-a-time process that is doable for anyone willing to make it happen.

Best of luck, and God bless!

Appendix
Resources and Business Form Templates

Forms

All the following practice forms are merely examples and are not the only or necessary way to create your documentation for your practice. Every provider will need to verify federal requirements and the state laws in which you practice as well as specific licensing regulations that may apply to each form. Readers are given permission to duplicate all or portions of these documents for personal use.

Forms

- Private Practice Checklist
- Intake Form (screening tool)
- Adolescent Informed Consent
- Teletherapy Informed Consent
- Policies and Consent for Treatment
- Client Insurance Information
- Notification of Fees/Good Faith Estimate
- Credit Card Authorization Form
- Superbill
- Release of Information
- Notice of Privacy Practices
- Monthly Business Profit-Loss Statement
- Initial Assessment (psychosocial)
- Initial Treatment Plan
- Fax Cover Sheet
- Return to School/Work Form

Private Practice Checklist

1. Name and brand your business
2. Decide what type of business model
   - sole proprietorship
   - LLC
   - S corp
   - C corp
   - partnership
   - secular versus Christian
   - generalist versus specialist
   - In person, telehealth, or hybrid
3. professional liability insurance
4. EIN (Employer Identification Number) or SSN
5. NPI
6. CAQH
7. office space
8. PO box versus office address
9. phone service
10. email
11. fax
12. insurance panels versus private pay
13. marketing
14. billing
15. electronic health record
16. setting fees
17. practice forms
18. business supplies and expenses

Intake Form

Name of Client: _____ Date Completed: _____

Date of Scheduled Intake: _____ Phone: _____

Are voice messages OK? Yes___ No ___

Are text messages OK? (For scheduling) Yes ___ No ___

Email: _____

Mailing Address: _____

DOB: _____ Age: _____ In Person _____

Telehealth _____ Both _____

Marital Status: _____ Gender: _____

Occupation: _____

Referral Source: _____

Reason for seeking treatment:

_____

_____

Have you had previous treatment? Yes ___ No ___ If so, when and where?

_____

Emergency Contact

Name: _____ Relationship to you: _____

Phone Number: _____ Address: _____

_____

City, State: Zip code:

What are you hoping to get out of coming to treatment?

_____

_____

Is there anything you would like your assigned intake therapist to know prior to attending your initial assessment?

_____

Policies and Consent for Treatment

Please initial after section to indicate you have read, understand, and agree.

Professional Services
(Name) provides professional services to individuals, families, couples, and groups. Please review the enclosed *Notification of Fees/ Financial Services Agreement* for billing rates, payment policies, and methods for collecting fees for services. Fees for services are expected by the conclusion of each session to avoid late fees/servicing fees being assessed to your account and/or suspension of services. Anyone carrying a balance of _____on their account is subject to these penalties until their balance is paid. Any outstanding *no- show fee/late-cancellation fee* will result in termination of services until the balance on the account is paid. These policies are put in place to protect the therapeutic relationship. **I do not provide expert witness, expert testimony, or custody evaluation services**. Do not ask or have your attorney subpoena my presence in court as I do not provide these services. If I am subpoenaed on your behalf, any and all preparation time, travel expenses/time, and court time will be billed to you at the rate of ____ plus actual incurred expenses to include but not limited to car rentals, airline tickets, hotels, meals, office supplies, consultation fees, legal expenses, missed work time, etc. You agree to this by signing this document.

_____ Please initial.

Confidentiality Policy
Within the limits described below, the information provided to me throughout the course of our professional relationship will be kept confidential and will not be disclosed without your consent. However, certain legal and ethical exceptions do require that confidentiality be broken and that information be disclosed under the following conditions:

- if you present a danger to yourself
- if you present a danger to someone else
- if there is a suspicion of child or elder abuse (or a vulnerable adult)
- if a legitimate subpoena/court order is issued
- if an insurance company requires information for reimbursement

_____ Please initial.

Payment for Services

Different copayments are required by various group coverage plans. Your copayment is determined by the mental health coverage policy selected by you and/or your employer. In addition, the copay may be different for the first visit than for subsequent visits. You are responsible for and shall pay your copay/coinsurance at the time that services are provided. It is recommended that you determine what your portion of the charged fees is *prior* to your first visit by calling your benefits office or insurance company. In the event that disclosure of your records or testimony is required by law, you will be responsible for the costs in producing both records and testimony at your therapist's current hourly rate at the time of the subpoena. Such payments are to be made prior to services being rendered by the therapist. A minimum retainer will be collected as a percentage of expected cost to be no less than __ for court appearances and/or deposition testimony.

_____ Please initial.

Appointments

Appointments can be scheduled or canceled via phone call, text, or email. The schedule line is _____, and the office email is _____ . Sessions are scheduled for approximately fifty minutes in length, including any administrative tasks that need to be accomplished (therapeutic hour). If you require additional time beyond what can be billed to your insurance or EAP (employee assistance plan), *you will be charged for the additional time at the full hourly rate (prorate)*. If you experience an emergency after hours, you can call 911, go to your local emergency room, or call **crisis mental health services** for _____ **at** _____. I am available by text, but I cannot guarantee that I will always be immediately accessible and should not be relied upon for crisis situations. **A twenty-four-hour notice (noon the day prior to your appointment) is required for changes to your reserved/scheduled appointment time** to avoid a *late-cancellation/ no-show fee*. This fee is not reimbursable by your insurance company or EAP. Your credit card on file will be automatically charged for the *no-show*. If your card is declined and you do not attend to your balance within thirty days, your chart will be closed due to violation of this agreement and services will be terminated. **These fees/ policies apply as soon as you have reserved your first session**. If your appointment is on a Monday, you must cancel your session by noon on Friday to avoid a no-show/late-cancel fee.

_____ Please initial.

Number and Length of Appointments

The number of therapy sessions needed to help you achieve your therapy goals depends on many factors and should be discussed with your provider. Most sessions are forty-five to fifty minutes in length but will be longer for the initial assessment in most cases. There are times that your therapist may suggest shorter sessions for clinical reasons. Appointments are made or canceled by texting the appointment line at ___. If you prefer to email, you can do this at ___. Text and email requests are responded to ___. Requests made outside of these hours may not be honored and may be subject to fees. By utilizing any electronic form of communication, you take on any risk associated with that form of communication as it pertains to confidentiality. (Name) does make every effort to protect privacy and contracts with providers who advertise that they do the same through high levels of encryption. (Name) does password protect all devices used to store any

PHI (protected health information), including phones and computers. Most databases and web sites used are accessed through a two-step authentication process as well. If this is a concern, please speak to your provider so that alternatives can be planned.

_____ Please initial.

Email/Electronic Communication

Please be advised that any communication delivered or stored electronically (via computer, email, phone, fax, and/or text) may not be completely secure or HIPAA compliant. This could result in unforeseen limits on privacy. In addition, electronic forms of communication, including email, may be added to your medical record. (Name) makes every attempt to contract with providers who are HIPAA compliant.

_____ Please initial.

Illness Policy

At times you and/or your provider (or her family) may become ill, resulting in a need for a change in your scheduled appointment time. Your therapist asks that you provide as much notice as possible under these circumstances, and she will do the same. If you notify your therapist that you are ill or need to miss a session due to the illness of a family member, you will not be charged for the missed session so long as you contact (name) the morning of the scheduled appointment. If you miss your session due to illness but do not notify your therapist the morning of, you will receive a *no-show/late-cancel* charge. If missing sessions due to illness becomes habitual, your therapist reserves the right to charge your account a *sick-cancel fee* of $25–$50. This is quite rare and only occurs when excessive absences disrupt both the client's care and your therapist's ability to assign your reserved time slot to other clients on a regular basis.

_____ Please initial.

Client-Therapist Relationship

The therapist-client relationship is limited to being professional and therapeutic. (Name) does not accept requests to become "friends" on any social media platforms with current or former clients. Any requests will be ignored. Please do not message your therapist through social media. This boundary is established so that roles are clearly defined to ensure professionalism and confidentiality is maintained.

_____ Please initial.

Terminating Therapy

Treatment is typically terminated when it becomes reasonably clear that the client no longer needs care. In general, therapy sessions are tapered down gradually (i.e., weekly to biweekly to monthly, etc.) with the knowledge and cooperation of the client. (Name) reserves the right to discontinue the therapeutic relationship if she believes that she is unable to provide effective/ethical treatment given the unique needs of the client. Treatment may also be terminated if the client consistently refuses to follow the recommendations of (name) and/or the treatment team that are critical to maintaining safety and/or standards of care (for instance a recommendation to a higher level of care or a medical/psychiatric evaluation or care). If the client routinely misses scheduled appointments (no-shows/late cancellations three or more times within a six-month period or goes more than thirty days without contacting the therapist regarding absence/no contact), treatment may be terminated. (Name) may terminate treatment if she is threatened or otherwise endangered or abused by the client or anyone related to or accompanying the client to treatment. There is a *no-tolerance* policy regarding behaviors that are disrespectful, devaluing, threatening, or otherwise inappropriate toward the provider, other providers, or other clients or persons in the building at any time. Misrepresentation or omission of pertinent clinical information is also grounds for termination. Whenever possible, pretermination counseling and referrals for alternate services/providers will be offered.

_____ Please initial.

Risks of Therapy
Therapy is the Greek word for "change." One risk of therapy is that you may learn things about yourself (or a family member/partner) that you do not like. You may feel emotionally uncomfortable at times since growth often occurs when one experiences and confronts issues that induce sadness, sorrow, anxiety, or pain. After making changes in your thinking and/or behaviors, your friends and family may respond differently to you, and it is impossible to predict their response. One risk of marital therapy, for example, is the risk of separation or divorce after reaching greater insight.

_____ Please initial.

Limitations to Couples/Family Therapy
Couples/family counseling will be most impactful in cases where all parties put in a good faith effort to improve their relationships. All members of a couple/family must be present and on time for the session to take place unless previously determined otherwise by the therapist and family/couple. If members are late/absent, the session will not take place and the session will be billed and documented as a no-show/late cancel. Deliberate dishonesty or deceit, unwillingness to look at oneself and take responsibility for one's actions, or lack of interest and motivation to engage in treatment by one or more parties will undermine the therapeutic process. The couple or family is the client. The medical records belong to the couple or the family. This means that, except for in the circumstances described under the confidentiality policy, all adults will have to consent to any release of records or information to a third party. At times, the entire group/couple will be seen together. Other times, your therapist may determine that one individual or another may benefit from

being seen alone by either (name) or another provider. This will be discussed by all parties. In general, there is a *no-secrets* policy in family/couples counseling. Your therapist will not promise to keep secrets from other members of the group. This is especially true if the secret is harmful or destructive to the therapeutic process or undermines mutually agreed-upon treatment goals. *When/if a family member is seen individually as a part of family/couples counseling, these records remain in the family/couples chart unless the individual has established themselves as an individual client.*

_____ Please initial.

Treatment of Minors

Adolescents are entitled to privacy and their sessions will remain private. Parents are asked to waive their right to access records to facilitate trust between their minor child and the therapist. Without trust that what they are saying will remain confidential, many minors will not be honest during therapy sessions. There are some exceptions to confidentiality that apply to what is shared in the sessions of minors that mirror those of adults, such as reporting harm to self or others or a court order/insurance company request for records. Also reporting that harm is coming to them confidentiality will be broken as mandated reporters are required to do so. This is outlined further in the adolescent/child consent form.

_____ Please initial.

By signing below, you acknowledge that you have reviewed the policies above and consent to the above terms. You are agreeing to initiate treatment (or give consent for your minor child to participate in care) with (name) via in-person ___, telehealth ___, or a combination ___ of the two forms of counseling services. (Please check the modes you consent to currently.)

_____   _____
Client's Signature   Date

Adolescent Informed Consent

Parent Agreement to Respect Privacy

The purpose of seeing a counselor is to get help with problems that are bothering you or keeping you from being successful in your life. Whether you asked to speak with a counselor or your parents, teachers, school counselors, doctors, or someone else suggested you come, I am excited to have the opportunity to work with you. The process of counseling involves getting to know your perspective on some of the difficulties in your life and in some instances discovering better ways to manage them.

Sometimes these difficulties will include topics you do not want your parents or guardians to know about. For most people, knowing that what they say will be kept private helps when discussing thoughts, feelings, and perceptions and to have more trust in their therapist. As a teenager, you have rights that are not equal to those of an adult (a person eighteen years old), but privacy, or confidentiality, is an especially important part of therapy. You should also know that state law gives your parents/guardians the right to see any written record I keep about our sessions. It is rare that a parent/guardian would ever request to look at these records, and I strongly discourage parents from doing this.

The information you share in our sessions is confidential unless you give me permission to release it. There are exceptions to this rule that you need to understand before we begin counseling. In some situations, it is required by law or professional guidelines that information discussed in therapy be disclosed. Some of those situations are listed below. Most of these situations involve your protection or the protection of others from potential harm.

1. If you report having a plan to harm yourself, confidentiality can be broken to protect you.

2. If you report having a plan to harm someone else, confidentiality can be broken to protect the person.

3. If you are involved in activities that could cause harm to yourself or someone else, even if you do not intend to harm yourself or someone else, confidentiality can be broken.

4. If you report that you are being abused (physically, emotionally, or sexually) or that you have been abused in the past, the law requires that I report this to the social services.

5. If you are involved in a court case and a request is made for information about your therapy, information will be disclosed with your written consent unless the court requires that information be provided. If this occurs, you will be informed of the proceedings, and efforts to protect your confidentiality will be taken and discussed with you.

6. If you agree that information can be shared with a specific person or entity, then we will discuss the limits of what will be shared and how that information will be shared.

Parents/guardians will not be told specific things that you share in therapy except for as described above. This includes activities and behaviors that your parents/guardians may not approve of or may be upset by but that do not put you or others at risk for immediate harm. It may be important to let your parents know some information that is protected by confidentiality, and you may be encouraged to share that information. Part of my job as a therapist is to discuss this with you and to decide together the best way to communicate the information. Also, when meeting with your parents, I may sometimes describe problems in general terms, without using specifics, to help them know how to be more helpful. You are always free to ask me about the types of information that I would disclose. You could ask me in the form of "hypothetical situations," such as "If someone told you that they were doing_____, would you tell their parents?"

Other Treatment Providers

You may have other treatment providers that you are working with while you are in counseling with me. I reserve the right to speak freely with other treatment providers without a separate release of information on file as provided under HIPAA. To provide the best quality care for you, I need to have access to your teachers, school counselors, physicians, dietitians, and any other pertinent professionals on your treatment team. By signing below, you are giving me permission to contact these providers. You can rescind this permission at any time.

Adolescent's Signature _____ Date _____

Parent's Signature _____ Date _____

Adolescent Therapy Client

Signing below indicates that you have reviewed the policies described above and understand the limits to confidentiality. If you have any questions as we progress in counseling, please ask your therapist at any time.

Adolescent's Signature _____ Date _____

Parent/Guardian

Check boxes and sign below, indicating your agreement to respect your adolescent's privacy.

/___/ I will refrain from requesting detailed information about individual therapy sessions with my child. I understand that I will be provided with periodic updates about general progress and/or may be asked to participate in therapy sessions as needed.

/___/ I know I have the legal right to request written records of my minor child, but I agree *not* to request these records to respect the confidentiality of my adolescent's treatment.

/___/ I understand that I will be informed about situations that could endanger my child. I know this decision to breach confidentiality in these circumstances is up to the therapist's professional judgment.

Parent's/Guardian's Signature _____ Date _____

Parent's/Guardian's Signature _____ Date _____

Therapist's Signature _____ Date _____

Teletherapy Informed Consent Form

The purpose of this consent is to give permission to engage in an adjunct form of treatment. _____ utilizes the _____ program, which incorporates network and software security protocols to protect the confidentiality of patient identification and imaging data and includes measures to safeguard the data and to ensure its integrity against intentional or unintentional corruption. _____ is HIPAA compliant.

I hereby consent to engage in teletherapy with _____. Teletherapy is a form of psychological service provided via secure internet technology, which can include consultation, treatment, transfer of medical data, emails, telephone conversations, and/or education using interactive audio, video, or data communications. I also understand that teletherapy involves the communication of my medical/mental health information, orally and/or visually.

Teletherapy has the same purpose or intention as psychotherapy or psychological treatment sessions that are conducted face-to-face at the office of _____. However, due to the nature of the technology used, I understand that teletherapy may be experienced somewhat differently from face-to-face treatment sessions.

I understand that I have the following rights with respect to teletherapy:

Client's Rights, Risks, and Responsibilities

1. I, the client, need to be a resident of _____. (This is a legal requirement for counselors practicing in this state under a/ an _____ license.) If I will not be residing in either state during teletherapy treatment, I will need to inform _____ of this change.

2. I, the client, have the right to withhold or withdraw consent at any time without affecting my right to future care or treatment.

3. The laws that protect the confidentiality of my medical information also apply to teletherapy. As such, I understand that the information disclosed by me during my therapy or consultation is confidential. However, there are both mandatory and permissive exceptions to confidentiality, which are discussed in detail in the general consent for treatment form I received at the start of psychotherapy treatment with _____.

4. I understand that there are risks and consequences from teletherapy, including but not limited to the possibility, despite best efforts to ensure secure technology on the part of,_____, that the transmission of my information could be disrupted or distorted by technical failures, the transmission of my information could be interrupted by unauthorized persons, and/or the electronic storage of my medical information could be accessed by unauthorized persons.

5. There is a risk that services could be disrupted or distorted by unforeseen technical problems.

6. In addition, I understand that teletherapy-based services and care may not be as complete as face-to-face services. I also understand that if _____ believes I would be better served by another form of therapeutic services (e.g., face-to-face services), I will be referred to a professional who can provide such services in my area if there are therapists who continue to provide face-to-face services at this time.

7. I understand that I may benefit from teletherapy but that results cannot be guaranteed or assured. I understand that there are potential risks and benefits associated with any form of psychotherapy and that despite my efforts and the efforts of my counselor, my condition may not improve, and in some cases, it may even get worse.

8. I accept that teletherapy does not provide emergency services. If I am experiencing an emergency, I understand that I can call 911 or proceed to the nearest hospital emergency room for help. If I am having suicidal thoughts or making plans to harm myself, I can call the National Suicide Prevention Lifeline at 1-800-273-TALK (8255) for free, twenty-four-hour hotline support or the 988 mental health hotline. Clients who are actively at risk of harm to self or others are not suitable for teletherapy services. If this is the case or becomes the case in future, _____ will recommend more appropriate services.

9. I understand that there is a risk of being overheard by anyone near me if I am not in a private room while participating in teletherapy. I am responsible for (1) providing the necessary computer, telecommunications equipment, and internet access for my teletherapy sessions; (2) the information security on my computer; and (3) arranging a location with sufficient lighting and privacy that is free from distractions or intrusions for my teletherapy session. It is the responsibility of the treatment provider to do the same on their end.

10. I understand that dissemination of any personally identifiable images or information from the telemedicine interaction to researchers or other entities shall not occur without my written consent.

11. I understand that I have a right to access my medical information and copies of medical records in accordance with _____ law.

I have read, understand, and agreed to the information provided above:

Client's Signature _____ Date _____

Therapist's Signature _____ Date _____

Client Insurance Information

Client Name: _____ Date of Birth: _____

Gender: Male ____ Female ____ Other ____

SSN: _____ Cell Phone Number: _____
Address: _____
_____
City   State   Zip Code

Client's Relationship to Subscriber:
Self ____ Spouse ____ Child ____ Other _____

Client's Status: Single ____ Married ____ Cohabitating ____
                 Separated ____ Divorced ____ Other _____
                 Employed ____ Unemployed ____
                 Full-Time Student ____ Part-Time Student ____

Name of Insurance Carrier: _____
Insurance Company's Phone Number: _____

Primary Subscriber's Name: _____ DOB _____
Subscriber's SSN: _____
Subscriber's Address: _____
_____
City   State   Zip Code

Subscriber's ID (**for Tricare only, DOD ID #**): _____
_____

Subscriber's group # (**for Tricare only, benefits #**):
_____

Subscriber's Employer or School _____

Effective Date: _____
Copay or coinsurance amount: $_____
Is there a deductible, and how much is it? _____
How much is remaining? _____
Is preauthorization required? _____
Preauthorization # _____

You must have a diagnosable condition for your insurance to be billed. If you do not attend your intake or if you do not have a diagnosable condition, you will be responsible for the cost of your intake session, which is ____. Your credit card will be charged for a *no-show/late cancel* for a missed intake appointment. For minors, if parents attend the first meeting of an intake and the minor child does not return for the intake, insurance cannot be billed and you will be responsible for the full fee ____. Clients cannot be diagnosed without attending their intake appointment.

Notification of Fees/Good Faith Estimate

Professional Services

Psychotherapy
Initial Assessment $_____
Individual Therapy (up to 30 minutes) $_____
Individual Therapy (up to 45 minutes) $_____
Individual Therapy (up to 60 minutes) $_____
Family/Couples Counseling $_____
Group Therapy $_____

Professional Services
Professional Coaching: Goal-Setting Session $_____
Professional Coaching Follow-Up Sessions $_____

Professional Consultation $_____

Supervision for Licensure   TBD

Additional Services
No-Show/Late-Cancellation Fee $_____
Sick Cancel Fee (See Illness Policy) $_____
Returned Check Fee $_____
Copies of Medical Record   According to state
                                                            law maximum
                                                            allowable fee

Meeting Attendance $_____
Court Appearance/Legal Proceeding ($500 retainer) $_____
Consult with Legal Representative $_____

By signing this form, you acknowledge receipt, understanding, and agreement to all applicable fees for services and a willingness to allow ___ to bill your commercial insurance plan for reimbursement and/or charge your credit card on file for any outstanding balances on your account.

_____   _____
Client's Signature   Date

*Fees are subject to change.

Credit Card Authorization Form

Cancellation of Appointments
To be respectful of the needs of all patients, please be courteous and contact your therapist if you are unable to attend your scheduled appointment *at least twenty-four hours* in advance of your reserved time slot. Appointment times are in high demand, and your early cancellation will allow other patients to access timely psychological care.

How to Cancel Your Appointment
To change or cancel your reserved appointment time, please call or text the appointment line at _____, or email your therapist at _____.

No-Show/Late Cancellation
A *no-show* is a patient who misses an appointment without canceling at least twenty-four hours prior to their reserved session time. Clients are expected to contact their therapist by *no later than noon on the day prior* to their scheduled appointment to allow for time to reallocate that session time to another client. A failure to be present at the time reserved for you or your family member will be recorded in the medical record as a *no-show* and will be automatically charged to the credit card on file accordingly. *This includes arriving at your scheduled appointment fifteen minutes or more past the scheduled start time.*

(Name) requires that *all* clients have a credit card on file to be used in the event of a no-show. The minimum fee for a no-show is ___. Your therapist cannot bill your insurance company for a no-show fee, so your charge will be for the *full fee* for the services missed due to a no-show. This practice of charging for no-shows/late cancellations is standard in the field and takes into account that you are not simply paying for services rendered but you are reserving a time slot your therapist will not be able to offer to someone else on short notice. The fee charged is for the time reserved for your service.

Please enter the card information you wish to keep in file for automatic deduction of session fees, no-show/late fees, copayments/coinsurance, and deductibles (if applicable). Only fees that have been previously disclosed to you and agreed to you per your intake consent forms will be charged without your permission.

Client Name _____

Cardholder's Information (Please include the name and address associated with the credit/debit card you wish to use.)

Cardholder Name _____
Address _____
City _____ State _____ Zip _____
Phone _____
Email _____

Credit/Debit Card Information
Card Type: Visa ___ Mastercard ___ Discover ___ AMEX ___
         HSA ___ (cannot be used for no-show fees) ___

*If using an HSA for cost of services, a credit/debit must also be on file for no-show/late-cancel fees. Please advise therapist of the need for a second form.

Card Number _____
Expiration Date _____ 3-digit code on back _____

I, the cardholder, authorize fees for service and fees for *no-show and/or late cancellations* to be assessed to the card listed above.

_____   _____
Cardholder's Signature   Date

Superbill

Business Name   Provider Name
Address   Phone
Address   Tax ID XX XXXXXXX

Services billed to:

Client Name:_____ Acct #:_____

Patient Information	Dates	
Policy Holder	Service	Diagnosis
SSN	Total Sessions	Charge for sessions
Street	Total charges	
City, State, Zip	Adjustments	
M F DOB	Payments	
Insurance Carrier	Prior balance	
Policy # Group #	Late charges	
Relationship to policy holder	Balance due	

Procedural Codes

90791 Diagnostic Interview	99071 Educational Materials (Books, Audio)
90832 Individual Therapy (approx. 30 min)	Special Reports
90834 Individual Therapy (approx. 45 minutes)	Court Testimony/Appearance
90837 Individual Therapy (approx. 60 minutes)	Unusual Travel
90846 Family/Couples w/o patient	Hospital Visit
90847 Family/Couples w/patient	Consultation/Professional Consult
90853 Group Therapy	Conjoint Therapy
90839 Crisis (30–74 minutes)	90830 (30 min additional crisis)
90837 + 99354 (90–134 minutes)	
90837+99354+99355 (135–164 minutes)	**Telephone Calls**
+99050 Services Outside Business Hours	Telephone Call, Straightforward (15 minutes)
+99051 Planned Evening, Weekend, Holiday	Intermediate (16–29 minutes)
+99355 Add-On	Moderate (30–45 minutes)
+99354 Add-On	Complex (46 minutes–60+)

Authorization to Release and Obtain Confidential Information

Client Name: _____
Date of Birth: _____

I hereby authorize _____ to receive () and/or to release () information obtained in the course of the diagnosis and treatment of the above-named client for mental health purposes from/to:

Name of Individual/Agency/Facility (indicate who you want your information released to or collected from):

_____
Phone:_____
Fax:_____
Address:_____
City:_____ State: _____Zip Code: _____

This authorization releases _____, its owner, and any of its employees or independent contractors from any legal responsibility or liability for the disclosure of the following information to the extent indicated and authorized herein. I hereby consent to the release of records pertaining to diagnosis and treatment of the following. (If client is a minor and information is to be released regarding treatment for alcohol or drug abuse, both the client and the parent/guardian must sign.)

Yes () No () Conditions related to drug and/or alcohol abuse

Yes () No () Conditions related to psychiatric/psychological treatment

Yes () No () Intake evaluation, diagnosis, recommendations, assessments, etc.

Yes () No () Progress notes, staffing notes, group notes, etc.

Yes () No () Discharge summary and/or verification of attendance

Yes () No () Lab reports or medical testing results

Yes () No () Other _____

Yes () No () No records. Two-way communication only for above marked items

Yes () No () Electronic communication (email, facsimile, etc.)

I understand I may revoke this consent at any time by contacting the above provider or facility. This consent will remain in effect unless I give my written revocation of consent. I understand that the release or transfer of the specified information to any person or entity not specified herein is prohibited. An additional written authorization must be obtained for a proposed new use of the information or for its transfer to another person or entity. I understand that I have the right to receive a copy of this authorization if I so request.

_____   _____
Client's Signature   Date

_____   _____
Client's/Parent's (Guardian's) Signature   Date

_____   _____
Witness's Signature   Date

Notice of Privacy Practices

This notice describes how medical and mental health information about you may be used and disclosed and how you can get access to this information. Please review it carefully.

Your counselor is dedicated to maintaining the privacy of your personal health information. We are required by law to protect this information, but we are also required by law to report some information. This notice of privacy practices (NPP) is a required, but abbreviated, explanation of how the law and regulations impact you. We cannot cover all aspects of the Health Insurance Portability and Accountability Act of 1996 (HIPAA) and the other federal and state laws and regulations that govern the use and limitations of use of your personal health information. Our policy is to give a minimum amount of information to protect you and to allow us to comply with the required duties. You are invited to discuss these matters with your therapist. Each time you visit a health care provider, you give information about your physical and mental health. In the law, this information is called protected health information (PHI). This information goes into your medical or health care record or file. With your written consent, the health care provider can use your PHI to provide treatment, process for payment, and administer health care operations.

Primary Uses and Disclosures of Protected Health Information

Treatment – Once you give consent and your treatment begins, the information you give us about you may be used confidentially for peer consultation or disclosed to other health care professionals for the purpose of evaluating your health, diagnosing mental health conditions, and providing treatment. We may also coordinate with your primary care doctor, registered dietitian, or another specialist who is treating you.

Payment – The information you give us about yourself may be used to seek payment from your health plan or from other sources of coverage, such as an automobile insurer or workers' compensation. For example, your health insurance company may request and receive information on dates of service, the services provided, and the diagnosis and symptoms of mental health condition being treated.

Business Associates – There are some jobs we hire other businesses to do. In the law, they are called business associates. These may include a billing service, an accountant, and/or an attorney. These business associates may need to receive some of your PHI to do their work properly. We will give these business associates the minimum amount of information to do their work. To protect your privacy, they have agreed in their contract with us to safeguard your information.

Additional Uses of Protected Health Information – The following is a description of some other possible ways in which we may (and are required or permitted by law to) use and/or disclose your protected health information. We will not use or share your information other than as described here unless you tell us we can in writing. If you agree we can, you may change your mind at any time by informing us in writing. If you pay for a service out of pocket in full, you can ask us not to share that information for the purpose of payment or our operations with your health insurer. We will comply with this request unless a law requires us to share that information.

Abuse or Neglect – As required or permitted by law, we may disclose your protected health information to a government authority that is authorized by law to receive reports of suspected abuse or neglect of a child or vulnerable adult. If feasible and appropriate, in our professional judgment, we will inform you of such a disclosure.

To Prevent a Serious Threat to Health or Safety – As required or permitted by law, we may disclose your protected health information if we believe that the disclosure is necessary to prevent a serious and imminent threat to the health or safety of a person or persons.

Law Enforcement – According to law, in some cases your information may be disclosed to law enforcement or social service agencies, without your explicit, written permission, to support government audits and inspections, to facilitate law enforcement investigations, and to comply with government mandated reporting. This may be done even if you pay out of pocket for services.

Public Health Reporting – The information you give us may be disclosed to public health agencies as required by law. These are agencies that investigate diseases and injuries.

Health Oversight Agencies – We may disclose your protected health information to health oversight agencies such as _____ Board of Behavioral Health Examiners as authorized by law.

Legal Proceedings – We may disclose your protected health information during a judicial or administrative proceeding, in response to an order of the court or a subpoena.

Research – We may use or share your information to do research to improve treatments when the research is approved by an institutional review board and follows established protocols to ensure the privacy of the information. In all these cases, your name, address, and other information that reveals who you are will be removed from the information given to the researchers.

For Government Functions – We may disclose protected health information of military personnel and veterans to government benefit programs relating to eligibility and enrollment, to workers' compensational programs, to correctional facilities, if you are an inmate, and for national security reasons.

The Secretary of the US Department of Health and Human Services – We are required to disclose your protected health information to the secretary of the US Department of Health and

Human Services when the secretary is investigating or determining our compliance with the HIPAA privacy regulations.

Others Involved in Your Health Care – With your written consent, we may disclose your protected health information to a friend or family member you have identified as being involved in your health care. We also may disclose our information to an entity assisting in a disaster relief effort so that your family can be notified about your condition, status, and location. In an emergency, if you are not present or able to agree to these disclosures of your protected health information, then we may, using our professional judgment, determine whether the disclosure is in your best interest. We may also share your information when needed to lessen a serious and imminent threat to health or safety.

Correspondence – Your information may be used by our staff to send you bills, a newsletter with information about our programs, and other correspondence. We do not release your name to others for mailing lists. Please advise the office if you do not wish to receive such mailings at your home address.

Disclosures to You – We are required to disclose to you most of your protected health information in a "designated record set" when you request access to this information. Generally, a "designated record set" contains medical and billing records, as well as other records that are used to make decisions about your health care benefits. We are also required to provide, upon your written request, an accounting of any disclosures of your protected health information that are for reason other than payment and health care.

Other Uses and Disclosures of Your Protected Health Information
Any other uses and disclosures of our protected health information that are not described above require your written authorization. If you change your mind after authorizing the use or disclosure of your information, you may submit a written revocation of the

authorization. This revocation will be effective immediately and in the future. However, the revocation will not be effective for information that we already have used or disclosed in reliance on your authorization. You may also revoke, in writing, your consent for treatment that would terminate your treatment with your counselor.

Your Rights

You have certain rights under the federal privacy standards. These include the following:

Right to Request a Restriction – You have a right to request a restriction on the protected health information we use or disclose about you for payment or health care operations. We are not required to agree to any restriction that you may request. If we do agree to the restriction, we will comply with the restriction unless the information is needed to provide emergency treatment to you and if it allows us to comply with the law. You may request a restriction by writing or completing our form for this purpose. In your request, tell us the information you want to limit and how you want to limit our use and/or disclosure of the information.

Right to Request Confidential Communications by Alternative Means – If you believe that a disclosure of all or part of your protected health information may endanger you, you may request that we communicate with you regarding your information in an alternative manner or at an alternative location. For example, you can request that we only contact you at work.

Right to Inspect and Copy – As permitted by federal regulation, we require that requests to inspect, copy, or release protected health information be submitted in writing to your counselor. If you request a copy of the information, we may charge a fee for the costs of copying, mailing, or other costs associated with your request. Please note that the law does not guarantee you the right of access to or possession of a mental health therapist's personal or psychotherapy notes. Your counselor may deny your request to inspect and copy your protected health information in certain limited circumstances. If you are denied access to your information, you may request that the denial be reviewed. A licensed health care professional chosen by us will review your request and the denial. The person performing this review will not be the same one who denied your initial request. Under certain conditions, our denial will not be reviewable. If this event occurs, we will inform you in our denial that the decision is not reviewable.

Right to Amend – If you believe that your protected health information is incorrect or incomplete, you may request in writing that we amend your information. Your written request should include the reason the amendment is necessary. In certain cases, we may deny your request for the amendment. If we deny your request, you have the right to file a statement of disagreement with us. Your statement of disagreement will be linked with the disputed information and all future disclosures of the disputed information will include your statement.

Right of an Accounting – You have a right to receive an accounting of most disclosures of your protected health information for reasons other than payment, treatment, or health care operations. This accounting will not include disclosures for which you provided an authorization. An accounting will include the date(s) of the disclosure but will not include disclosures made before January 1, 2012. We are permitted to charge you for the cost of producing the list.

Rights for Confidentiality in Substance Abuse Treatment – You may have additional rights of confidentiality under 42 CFR Part 2. Ask for a special authorization form if you wish.

Rights to Receive a Printed Copy of This Notice – You have a right to receive a printed copy of this notice.

Duties of Your Counselor – We are required by law to maintain the privacy of your protected health information and to provide you with this notice of privacy practices. We also are required to abide by the privacy policies and practices that are outlined in this notice. All members of our staff and business associates are under contract to respect your confidentiality and privacy as outlined in this notice. For security, your files are maintained and protected in a locked cabinet when not in use. We will let you know promptly if a breach may have compromised the privacy or security of your information. As permitted by law, we reserve the right to amend or modify our privacy policies and practices. These changes in our policies and practices may be required by changes in federal and state laws and regulations. Whatever the reason for these revisions, we will make available in our office a revised notice. The revised policies and practices will be applied to all protected health information that we maintain.

Complaints You also may file a complaint with the secretary of the US Department of Health and Human Services. Complaints filed directly with the secretary must (1) be in writing, (2) contain the name of the entity against which the complaint is lodged, (3) describe the relevant problems, and (4) be filed within 180 days of the time you became or should have become aware of the problem. The mailing address is Secretary of the Department of Health and Human Services, Office for Civil Rights, US Department of Health and Human Services, Room 509F, HHH Building, 200 Independence Avenue, SW, Washington, DC, 20201. The phone number is 1-800-368-1019. The email address is ocrprivacy@ hhs.gov, or visit the web site at www.hhs.gov/ocr/privacy/hipaa/ complaints/. You will not be penalized or otherwise retaliated against for filing such a complaint.

Please sign to acknowledge reading this document regarding your therapist's privacy practices.

_____   _____
Signature   Date

Monthly Business Profit-Loss Statement

Receipts and Disbursements for Month End _____

Date Prepared_____

Gross Receipts		**Monthly Total:**
1 Gross Sales		$_____
2 Less Cost of Goods Sold (Refunds)		$_____
3 Gross Profit (subtract line 2 from 1)		$_____
4 Add Other Income		$_____
5 **Gross Income** (add lines 3 and 4)	A	$_____

Business Costs and Expenses		
6 Business Property Rent/Lease		$_____
7 Business Property Utilities		$_____
8 Salaries/Wages (not included in line 2; exclude owner's draw)		$_____
9 Employee Benefits		$_____
10 Payroll Tax Deposits		$_____
11 Sales Tax Deposits		$_____
12 Other Tax Deposits		$_____
13 Auto Expense		$_____
14 Repairs/Maintenance		$_____
15 Insurance on Business (Fire, Theft, Liability, etc.)		$_____
16 Workman's Comp Insurance		$_____
17 Supplies (not included in line 2)		$_____
18 Telephone/Internet/Fax		$_____
19 Advertising/Promotion		$_____
20 Travel/Entertainment		$_____
21 Professional Fees Paid (Attorney, Accountant)		$_____
22 Professional Memberships		$_____
23 Professional Licenses		$_____
24 Educational Expenses		$_____
25 Other Costs/Expenses_____		$_____
26 **Total Business Costs and Expenses for Month**	B	$_____

27 **Net Income (Loss) for Month (A minus B)**		$
		=============

Total Funds on Hand at End of Month	$_____
Total Inventory on Hand at End of Month	$_____
Total Accounts Receivable (Collectable) at End of Month	$_____
Total Accounts Payable at End of Month	$_____

Initial Assessment

Name: _____ Gender: _____
Date of Birth: _____/_____/_____ Date of Intake: ____/____/____
Marital Status _____ Race/Ethnicity: _____

Presenting Complaint

_____

History of Present Illness

_____
_____
_____

Past Psychiatric/Psychological History

_____
_____
_____
_____
_____
_____
_____
_____

History of Chronic Illnesses, Injuries, Conditions, Disabilities

_____
_____
_____

Past Surgical History

_____
_____
_____

Allergies _____

Current Medication List

Medication	Dose	Frequency	Reason	Prescriber

Past Medication List

Medication	Dose	Frequency	Reason Started	Reason Stopped

Counseling Issues (Check All That Apply)

__ abortion

__ anger management

__ attention issues

__ body image

__ decision-making

__ divorce/separation

__ eating disorder

__ fertility/infertility issues

__ hallucinations (auditory, visual

__ homicidal feelings

__ legal issues

__ loneliness/social isolation

__ peer relationships

__ academic performance

__ anxiety

__ behavior issues

__ career/transition

__ depression

__ drug/alcohol abuse

__ family relationships

__ grief/loss

__ hair pulling

__ learning disability

__ LGBTQ+

__ OCD

__ postpartum depression

___ pregnancy (past/present)   ___ rape
___ self-confidence/self-esteem   ___ sexual abuse
___ sleep problems/nightmares   ___ stress
___ spirituality   ___ suicidal feelings
___ other _____

Eating Disorders Assessment

Has client ever been diagnosed with an eating disorder? Yes___ No___

___ anorexia   ___ bulimia   ___ binge-eating D/O
___ OSFED   ___ ARFID   ___ rumination D/O
___ pica   ___ orthorexia   ___ diabulimia

Previous Treatment? When? Where?

_____

_____

Height: _____ Weight: _____
Highest Weight: _____ Lowest Weight: _____
SIV: _____ Laxatives: _____
Diuretics: _____ Diet Pills: _____
Binging: _____ Overexercise: _____
Diet History: _____

Age of Menarche: _____ Amenorrhea: _____
Abnormal Periods: _____
   Date of Last Lab Draw: _____ Date of Last Physical: _____
Oral Contraceptives: _____ Dexa Scan: _____

Current Physical Activity: _____

Current Eating Habits (kcal/d):_____

_____

Drug/Alcohol Assessment

Which substances do you use? Method of use? Frequency? Time period of use? Used in the past?

__ alcohol				__ alcohol	
__ caffeine				__ caffeine	
__ nicotine				__ nicotine	
__ heroin				__ heroin	
__ opiates				__ opiates	
__ marijuana				__ marijuana	
__ cocaine/crack				__ cocaine/crack	
__ methamphetamines				__ methamphetamines	
__ inhalants				__ inhalants	
__ stimulants				__ stimulants	
__ hallucinogens				__ hallucinogens	
__ other:				__ other:	

Suicidal/Homicidal Ideation

Is there a suicide risk? ____ No ____ Yes

Was there a previous attempt? ____ No ____Yes (If yes, when? _____)

Current plan ____ Means to carry out plan ____ Intent ____ Lethality of plan? Is the patient dangerous to others? ____ Yes ____ No

Does the patient have thoughts of harming others? ____ Yes ____ No (If yes: Identify target): _____

Can the thoughts of harm be managed? ____ Yes ____ No ____

Current plan ____ Means to carry out plan ____ Intent ____ Lethality of plan

High-risk behaviors ____ None ____ Cutting ____ Anorexia/Bulimia ____ Head banging ____ Self-injurious behaviors ____ Other: _____

Abuse Assessment

In the past year, has the client been hit, kicked, or physically hurt by another person?

_____

_____

_____

Is the client in a relationship with someone who threatens or physically harms them?

_____

_____

_____

Has the client been forced to have sexual contact that they were not comfortable with?

_____

_____

_____

Has the client ever been abused? ____ Yes ____ No

If yes, describe by whom, when and how.

_____

_____

_____

_____

_____

_____

Family/Social History

Where was client born/raised? _____

Siblings ____ # of brothers ____ # of sisters

What was the birth order? ____ of ____ children

Who primarily raised the patient? _____

Members of Current Household

Name	Age	Gender	Relationship

Describe marriages or significant relationships:

_____

Number of children: _____

Current living situation:

_____

Military history/type of discharge:

_____

Support/social network:

_____

Significant life events:

_____

Family History of Mental Illness

_____

_____

_____

_____

_____

_____

_____

Employment

What is the current employment status? _____

Does the client like their job? _____

Describe relationships with coworkers? _____

Does the patient perform well at their job? _____

Has the client ever been fired? Yes ____ No ____

If yes, explain.

_____

_____

How many jobs has the client had in the last five years? _____

Education

Highest grade completed: _____

Schools attended: _____

Discipline problems: _____

Current Legal Status

_____ No legal problems _____ Parole _____ Probation _____
Charges pending _____ Previous jail

Developmental History

Describe the childhood: ___ Traumatic ___ Painful ___ Uneventful

Describe the childhood in relation to personality, school, friends, and hobbies: _____

_____

_____

_____

_____

Describe any traumatic experiences in the childhood, Including ages.

_____

_____

_____

_____

What is the patient's sexual orientation? ___ Heterosexual ___
Homosexual ___ Bisexual

Spiritual Assessment

Religious/faith background: _____

Does the client currently attend any religious services? Yes ___ No
___ If yes, where?

_____

_____

_____

Does the client consider their religious/faith background to be an integral part of their life? Explain.

_____

_____

_____

Cultural Assessment

List any important issues that have affected the ethnic/cultural background.

_____

_____

_____

_____

Financial Assessment

Describe the financial situation.

_____

_____

_____

_____

_____

_____

Coping Skills

Describe how the client copes with stressful situations.

_____

_____

_____

_____

_____

Are the client's coping methods ____ adaptive ____ maladaptive?

Interests and Abilities

What hobbies does the client have?

_____

_____

_____

_____

What are the client's strengths?

_____

_____

_____

_____

What does the client enjoy?

_____

_____

_____

_____

Mental Status Assessment

WNL unless otherwise specified _____

Arousal/Orientation: _____ Alert _____ Sleepy _____ Attentive _____
Unresponsive _____

Oriented to person _____ Oriented to place _____ Oriented to time _____
Confused _____ Other: _____

Appearance:

_____ Well-groomed _____ Good eye contact _____ Poor eye contact _____
Disheveled _____ Bizarre _____ Poor hygiene _____ Inappropriate dress
_____ Other: _____

Behavior/Motor Activity:

_____ Normal _____ Restless _____ Agitated _____ Lethargic _____
Abnormal facial expressions _____ Tremors _____ Tics _____ Other:
_____

Mood/Affect:

_____ Normal _____ Depressed _____ Flat _____ Euphoric _____
Anxious _____ Irritable _____ Liable _____ Indifferent _____ Careless
_____ Inability to sense emotions _____ Lack of sympathy _____ Other:
_____

Speech:

_____ Normal _____ Nonverbal _____ Slurred _____ Soft _____ Loud _____
Pressured _____ Limited _____ Incoherent _____ Halting _____ Rapid _____
Other: _____

Attitude:

___ Cooperative ___ Uncooperative ___ Guarded ___ Suspicious
___ Hostile ___ Other: _____

Thought Process:

___ Intact ___ Flight of ideas ___ Tangential ___ Concrete thinking ___ Loose associations ___ Unable to think abstractly ___ Circumstantial ___ Neologisms ___ Racing ___ Word Salad ___ Other: _____

Thought Content:

___ Normal ___ Phobia ___ Hypochondriasis ___ Delusions ___ Obsessive ___ Preoccupations ___ Other: _____

Delusions:

___ None ___ Religious ___ Persecutory ___ Grandiose ___ Somatic ___ Ideas of reference ___ Thought broadcasting ___ Thought insertion ___ Other: _____

Hallucinations:

___ None ___ Auditory hallucinations ___ Visual hallucinations ___ Command hallucinations ___ Other: _____

Describe:

_____
_____
_____
_____
_____
_____

Impulse Control:

____ Normal ____ Partial ____ Limited ____ Poor ____

Is the client able to meet their basic needs? (e. g., food, shelter, medical): ____ Yes ____ No ____ If no, describe:

_____

_____

_____

_____

_____

_____

Functional Ability:

Check the area of concern ____ None ____ Activities of daily living ____ Work ____ Finances ____ School ____ Family relationships____ Social relationships ____ Safety ____ Legal ____ Cognitive functioning ____ Physical health ____ Housing ____ Impulse control ____ Social skills

Return to School/Work

Name of Client_____

I last saw _____ in my office on
_____ at _____ a.m./p.m.

_____ He/She is able to return to work/school today.

_____ He/She is *not* able to return to work/school today.

_____ He/She is able to return to work/school on a (full-time part-time modified) scheduled basis.

_____ He/She should be excused from work/school for _____
_____ days/weeks.

_____ He/She should be excused from PE class for _____
_____ days/weeks.

_____ He/She will require a minimum of _____ hours of treatment/week for the next _____ months and will need to be excused from work/school as appointments are not available outside of normal business hours.

_____   _____
Clinician's Signature   Date

Initial Treatment Plan

Client Name _____

Date _____ DOB _____

Primary Diagnosis: _____

Goals	Interventions	Frequency/Modality
__ Mood Stabilization	__ Psychiatric Consultation __ CBT __ DBT __ Physical Activity __ Socialization	__ Weekly __ Biweekly __ Ea. 3 weeks __ Monthly __ Individual __Family __ IOP/IP
__ Anxiety/ OCD Reduction	__ Psychiatric Consultation __ CBT __ DBT __ ERP__ Physical Activity __ Socialization	__ Weekly __ Biweekly __ Ea. 3 weeks __ Monthly __ Individual __Family __ IOP/IP
__ Decrease EDO Symptoms	__ Psychiatric Consultation __ CBT __ DBT __ ERP__ IOP __ IP __ Body Image Work __ RD Referral __ FBT __ FT __Therapeutic Meals	__ Weekly __ Biweekly __ Ea. 3 weeks __ Monthly __ Individual __Family __ IOP/IP
__ Decrease Trauma Symptoms	__ Psychiatric Consultation __ CBT __ DBT __ ERP__ Grounding Skills __ Strengthen Power, Voice, Trust __ Boundaries	__ Weekly __ Biweekly __ Ea. 3 weeks __ Monthly __ Individual __Family __ IOP/IP
__ Improve Relationships	__ Communication Skills __ FT __ Couples' Counseling __ Boundary Setting	__ Weekly __ Biweekly __ Ea. 3 weeks __ Monthly __ Individual __Family __ IOP/IP
__ Eliminate Self-Injurious Behaviors	__ DBT __ Psychoeducation __ DBT Group __ Psychiatric Consultation __ MD/NP Body Checks	__ Weekly __ Biweekly __ Ea. 3 weeks __ Monthly __ Individual __Family __ IOP/IP

__ Reduce ADHD Symptoms	__ Psychiatric Consult __ CBT __ __ Parent Coaching __ Time Management __ Organization Skills __ Psychoeducation	__ Weekly __ Biweekly __ Ea. 3 weeks __ Monthly __ Individual __Family __ IOP/IP
__ Improve Sleep Hygiene	__ Psychiatric Consult __ Maintain HS Routine __ Relaxation __ Stress Management __ Nutrition and Exercise __ Sleep Logs	__ Weekly __ Biweekly __ Ea. 3 weeks __ Monthly __ Individual __Family __ IOP/IP
__ Improve Parenting Skills	__ Coparenting Curriculum __ Psychoeducation __ FT	__ Weekly __ Biweekly __ Ea. 3 weeks __ Monthly __ Individual __Family __ IOP/IP
__ Increase Coping Skills	__ DBT __ Psychoeducation	__ Weekly __ Biweekly __ Ea. 3 weeks __ Monthly __ Individual __Family __ IOP/IP
__ Improve Self-Worth	__ Affirmation Work __ Positive Self-talk __ Spiritual Work/Faith-Based Counseling	__ Weekly __ Biweekly __ Ea. 3 weeks __ Monthly __ Individual __Family __ IOP/IP
__ Process Grief/Loss	__ Psychoeducation __ Writing Assignments __ Identify/Process Emotions __ Grief Support Groups	__ Weekly __ Biweekly __ Ea. 3 weeks __ Monthly __ Individual __Family __ IOP/IP
		__ Weekly __ Biweekly __ Ea. 3 weeks __ Monthly __ Individual __Family __ IOP/IP
		__ Weekly __ Biweekly __ Ea. 3 weeks __ Monthly __ Individual __Family __ IOP/IP

Client's Signature _____ Date _____
Clinician's Signature _____ Date _____

Fax Cover Sheet

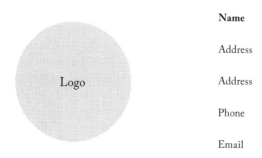

Name

Address

Address

Phone

Email

Fax

To: **From:**

Fax: **Fax:**

Phone: **Phone:**

No. Pages: **Date:**

Subject:

Comments:

NOTICE and DISCLAIMER: There is no guarantee of confidentiality through email and/or facsimile transmissions. The information in this fax may be PRIVILEGED and CONFIDENTIAL under one or more of the following state and federal laws: ARS § 36-445, ARS § 36-2403, Health Care Quality Improvement Act of 1986, Patient Safety and Quality Improvement Act of 2005, HIPAA legislation and/or the Electronic Communications Privacy Act. The information herein is intended only for the person(s) or entity(ies) to which it is addressed. Any review, retransmission, dissemination, or other use of this information by persons or entities other than the intended recipient(s) is prohibited. If you received this communication in error, please notify the sender above, and then delete or destroy all material immediately. Unless you are the intended recipient or his/her representative, you are not authorized to, and must not, read, copy, distribute, use, or retain this message or any part of it. Thank you.

References

Electronic Health Records

Simple Practice
https://www.simplepractice.com/

TheraNest
https://theranest.com

Therapy Notes
https://www.therapynotes.com/

TheraPlatform
https://www.theraplatform.com/

Online Resources

HIPAA (Health Insurance Accountability and Portability Act)
Summary of the HIPAA Privacy Rule | HHS.gov

(Good Faith Estimates/No Surprise Rules)
Ending Surprise Medical Bills | CMS

National Plan and Provider Enumeration System (NPPES) NPI
Application
https://nppes.cms.hhs.gov/

(CAQH) Council for Affordable Quality Healthcare Registration
www.proview.caqh.org

IRS Web Site
www.irs.gov

Web Site Builders

GoDaddy
https://www.godaddy.com/

Weebly
www.weebly.com

Wix
https://www.wix.com/

Marketing Materials

Vista Print
https://www.vistaprint.com/

Online Directories

Psychology Today
https://www.psychologytoday.com/us

Good Therapy
https://Goodtherapy.org

Therapy Tribe
https://www.therapytribe.com

Therapy Den
https://www.therapyden.com

Insurance Companies

Aetna
Anthem
Blue Cross/Blue Shield (Anthem)
Carefirst
ChampVA
Cigna
Humana
Kaiser
Magellan
MHN
Tricare
United Health Care

Credit Card Processing

Dharma Merchant Services
https://dharmamerchantservices.com/

Payment Cloud
https://paymentcloudinc.com/

Square
https://www.squareup.com

Telehealth Platforms

Capterra/Doxy.Me
https://www.capterra.com/

Secure Telehealth
https://securetelehealth.com/

Zoom (HIPAA-compliant version)
https://www.zoom.us

eSignature Products

DocuSign
https://go.docusign.com/trial/

Panda Doc
https://www.pandadoc.com/

Sign Now
https://www.signnow.com/

Glossary

Business associate agreement (BAA) – HIPAA regulations require that in each situation where PHI is exchanged or used between entities, a written agreement must be in place that is a legally binding contract called a BAA.

Certified eating disorders specialist (CEDS) – A licensed therapist or medical provider who has a significant amount of experience treating eating disorders in addition to completing high level training and passing an examination in the effective and collaborative treatment of feeding and eating disorders. This certification is granted by the International Association of Eating Disorders Professionals (IAEDP).

Council for Affordable Quality Healthcare (CAQH) – Online database that stores provider information. Insurance companies are granted access to this information to keep their provider directories current and updated.

Current procedural terminology (CPT codes) – Medical billing codes used to process medical billing claims.

Doing business as (DBA) – A name that a counselor has created for their practice other than their proper name.

Electronic health record (EHR) – An electronic version of a client's medical record that is maintained over time just as a written one. It may contain intake information, demographic information, progress notes, reports, discharge summaries, etc.

Employee assistance program (EAP) – A service provided through an employer. This program offers their employees free and confidential assessments and short-term counseling and/or referrals who are dealing with personal and/or work-related problems.

Health Insurance Portability and Accountability Act (HIPAA) – Federal law that restricts access to individuals' private health information.

International Classification of Diseases (ICD-10) – A set of designations used by health care staff to communicate elements of a patient's condition/diagnoses in a way that is universally accepted and recognized. The tenth and most recent edition is ICD-10.

Licensed professional counselor (LPC) – Master's-degreed mental health service providers licensed to practice mental health counseling services in the state(s) in which they hold a license.

National Plan and Provider Enumeration System (NPPES) – Web site to apply for an NPI.

National Provider Identifier (NPI) – A unique identification number for covered health care providers.

Occupational therapist (OT) – A form of therapy used for people recovering from physical or mental conditions that encourages rehabilitation through activities of daily living.

Primary care practitioner (PCP) – Medical providers that treat a wide array of health issues and can help coordinate your medical care with various specialists. A PCP may be a family physician, an internist, or a pediatrician.

Registered dietitian (RD) – An expert in food and nutrition who has earned a minimum of a bachelor's degree. RDs work in a wide array of employment settings and treat many different health conditions.

Superbill – A document for insurance carriers. They provide specific and detailed information about services a therapist or other health care professional provided to a client. Clients can then bill their insurance companies directly.

Acknowledgments

There are so many people that helped to make this book a reality.

I would first like to thank my family for your unconditional love and support. My children are the best cheerleaders and support staff a therapist and writer could ever want. The extra chores and cups of coffee retrieved while I worked on this project will never be forgotten. To my parents who always believed in me when others lost faith in my determination and abilities to see this and other projects through to the end. This one is for you, Mom.

I would also like to thank all my colleagues who assisted me along the way in growing my practice. A special shout-out to Michelle Rooker, LCSW, Kristen Bunger, RD, and the late Dr. Leslie Bond for all your support of me both personally and professionally. I would not be here without the compassion and kindness of friends and confidants in this business like all of you.

Thank you, and God bless everyone along the way who has given me strength and courage to reach for my dreams!

Printed in the United States
by Baker & Taylor Publisher Services